AF433654

Mom, Help Me!

Roadmap to Guiding Your Teen Away from Substance Use & Addiction

Nevriye A. Yesil

"Mom, Help Me!"

Roadmap to Guiding Your Teen Away from Substance Use & Addiction

Copyright © 2023. Nevriye A. Yesil. All rights reserved.

No part of this publication may be reproduced, distributed, or transmitted in any form or by any means, including, photocopying, recording, or other electronic or mechanical methods, without the prior written permission of the publisher, except in the case of brief quotations embodied in critical reviews and certain other noncommercial uses permitted by copyright law.

For permission requests, speaking inquiries, and bulk order purchase options, email info@brightwingsandcoco.com.

Bright Wings & Coco LLC
Brightwingsandcoco.com

Paperback ISBN:

Cover Design by Dani Popova

Edited by Robert Bolton

Disclaimer:

This book is for informational and educational purposes only and is not intended to treat, cure, or replace the professional treatment of a licensed counselor or practitioner for any disease or condition. Please consult with your healthcare professional before applying any recommendations provided in this book. The publisher and the author do not guarantee the accuracy and appropriateness of any suggestions shared in this book and are written to provide a basic guideline.

Printed in the United States.

Testimonials

"Reading 'Mom, Help Me!' was a game changer for me and my teenage daughter. We've grown so much closer since applying the advice and techniques shared in this book. Highly recommended for any parent navigating the often-turbulent teenage years!"

Samantha Jenkins,
mother of two, Atlanta, GA

"Nevriye Yesil provides a compassionate and insightful guide to understanding and supporting our teens as they face today's unique challenges. A must-read for any parent!"

David Nguyen,
father and educator, San Francisco, CA

"As a mom of three teenagers, I can't express enough how grateful I am for 'Mom, Help Me'. The practical tips and real-life scenarios have helped me strengthen my relationship with my children and better support them through their struggles. This book is a lifesaver!"

Karen Martinez,
proud mom, Austin, TX

"Raising well-rounded and emotionally healthy teenagers in today's environment can be challenging. 'Mom, Help Me' is the perfect guide for parents who want to ensure their children receive the support and understanding they need to thrive. I can't recommend this book enough!"

Sophia Kim,
investment banker and mother, New York City, NY

"Since reading 'Mom, Help Me', I've seen a huge improvement in my relationship with my teenage son. The book gave me the tools and understanding to effectively communicate with him and help him navigate through the challenges he faces. I can't recommend this book enough!"

Emily Thompson,
single mother, Boston, MA

"Teenagers can be a handful, but 'Mom, Help Me' by Nevriye Yesil makes it easier to understand and support them. The book is packed with helpful tips and advice that have made a real difference in my family's life. I'm so glad I picked this up!"

Steven Morales,
father of four, Tampa, FL

"'Mom, Help Me!' is an invaluable resource for any parent of teenagers. Nevriye Yesil's insightful guidance and advice have helped me connect with my daughter in ways I never thought possible. I truly believe this book has made me a better parent."

Victoria Sterling,
CEO and mother of two, Denver, CO

Dedication

To all the moms who are facing this heart-wrenching challenge, this book is for you. May the information and tools within these pages help you navigate your child to recovery and healing for all.

Table of Contents

Chapter Six
Breaking the Cycle of Addiction

Chapter Seven
Treatment Options and Recovery for Teens

Chapter Eight
Moving Forward

Conclusion

About the Author

References

Other Publications by the Author

INTRODUCTION

Do you have a teen child who is struggling with drug addiction? Do you want to help a loved one overcome addiction but do not know how? Would you like to know the treatment options? Are you wondering what you can do to help your child prevent a relapse? Or are you a mom in search of tips and guidance on how to prevent substance use in the first place? If you are looking for an answer to any of these questions, you are in the right place! I am here to help YOU help your loved one. Addiction is a double-edged sword, slicing into the hearts of both the substance user as well as their families. There is nothing more painful and devastating than watching your loved one struggle with addiction. In this book, I offer you a toolkit: a variety of insights and inspiration you will need to help your teen recover from substance use. The tools are here to help them reclaim their lives. From understanding the nature of drug addiction and its impact on the teen brain to treatment options and recovery, I will equip you in the coming chapters with the knowledge and skills you need to be the best advocate and ally for your teen.

This book is primarily written for you, Mom. You are the heart and soul of this book. I heard your voices, watched your struggles, and read your stories. It is a useful book for moms to navigate their teen child out of substance use and help them on the road to recovery. No question that moms and dads are equally important, and both play a critical role in raising their children. However, I believe a special bond between a mother and her child begins from the moment of conception. The direct physical connection before birth ties them together for life. Moms are traditionally the primary caregivers and are more involved in their child's day-to-day activities. This gives them a unique edge to know that something is off way before anybody else may even have a clue. I have witnessed firsthand how drugs can impact individuals and families. As I coached dozens of people and families in their journey to recovery, I also watched devasted moms bury their loved ones. As a mom myself, this experience had a profound impact on me and touched me deeply. I do not want this same thing to happen to you. My goal is to both educate and empower moms to manage this unique challenge more skillfully and with less fear and confusion. I believe with the right tools and guidance; you can help navigate your child out of addiction to a drug-free future full of possibilities.

While this book targets moms, anybody who is in the role of a primary caregiver, be it a father, aunt, or grandparent will find tremendous benefits from the information this book provides. It can also be a useful handbook for anyone who wants to know more about teen drug addiction: teachers, school counselors, relatives, other family members, and friends.

My journey and experience in the field of addiction started with incarcerated women. What initially began as part of a research project for my Ph.D. degree ended up becoming my passionate desire to support moms. A surprisingly large number of incarcerated women were moms and nearly all of them had families who were silently suffering alone. After spending countless hours interviewing and listening to their personal stories and collecting data, I began to see a pattern emerge. By reverse engineering, it became clear how this vulnerable population ended up using drugs. l gained insights, not only from their mistakes but also from the mistakes their families made, laying the foundation to engage in drug use. I also found myself in a unique position as a psychology instructor at a community college to have young students who sought my guidance with a range of challenges, including addiction. I had the privilege to earn their trust and the honor to provide the support they needed to quit. I have seen the struggles, challenges, and radical transformation of those I worked with. By drawing on the lessons I learned, I know with absolute certainty that there is hope.

Perhaps you are faced with this global challenge and feel desperate, hopeless, and helpless. In the midst of chaos and despair, I intend to turn your anger into compassion, confusion into determination, and hopelessness into hopefulness. You have what it takes to help your child to break free from substance use because within you is your biggest asset – the currency of a warrior's heart. Let this book be your compass and your inspiration to face this challenge with a heart full of courage and determination. I got your back. Hold my hand and let us walk this path together.

Tip: To make this book easy and fluid to read, I will simply use the word drugs. It includes all substances, legal and illegal as well as alcohol. I purposefully avoided details about each type of drug as you can simply google those facts. As you are reading this guide, drug lords and producers are probably experimenting in their garages or kitchens to find the next best drug with such interesting nicknames to hit the market that it makes it impossible to keep up. Regardless of what it is called, a drug is a drug.

Mom, Help Me!

The lion heart of a mom that

dares all things for the

love of her child.

Chapter One

UNDERSTANDING SUBSTANCE USE AND ADDICTION

1.1. Chaos of Drugs on the Teen Brain

Did you know that nearly 1 in 3 teens (29% of adolescents) have used some form of illegal drugs before they finish the 8th grade? And that 1 in 5 adolescents between the ages of 12 and 17 engage in problematic use of illicit drugs or alcohol. (The National Child Traumatic Stress Network 2008). Let that sink in for a minute! This global epidemic of substance use is killing people and ruining families. It is responsible for many premature deaths in America. Just in 2021 alone, more than 106,000 people died of a drug-related overdose (National Institute on Drug Abuse 2023). Astonishingly, that is one life lost approximately every 5 minutes. Behind every number are a tragic story, devasted families, and lives cut short. Unfortunately, an overdose is not always an accident. Intentional overdose is used by many as a form of suicide. According to research findings, while overall intentional drug overdose is on the decline nationwide, intentional overdose in 15–24-year old's is on the rise (Han et al. 2022). If your child expresses suicidal intentions or engages in self-harming behavior, take it seriously and immediately call the National Suicide Prevention Lifeline at 1-800-273-TALK (8255). Once more, this is a heartbreaking reminder of the power drugs can have on individuals and their dire consequences. To prevent such tragedies, we need to take a step back and look at the chaos and acknowledge the damage it can create in the brain.

The scientific community has helped broaden our understanding of how the brain works. While drug use has negative consequences for everybody of all ages, the use of drugs especially during adolescent years is a major concern. This is because the teen years are a sensitive period where significant physical, emotional, and cognitive changes are taking place. It is also a critical period for the brain. During this time, the brain is undergoing major neural changes in its structure and function and the process of maturation does, in fact, not finish until the mid to late 20s (National Institute of Mental Health 2020). Drugs can disrupt this process which can lead to long-term impairments and lasting damage to the developing brain and cognitive functions (Gould 2010). Here are four keyways in which drugs can affect and interfere with the brain's proper function:

1. **Structural Changes in the Brain:** It can affect and change brain function and structure in several brain regions leading to a variety of cognitive impairments (Vetreno et al,2017, Perez-Ramirez et al. 2017, Nicolas et al. 2017). With repeated use, drugs become hardwired in the brain and become a part of a person's 'biologically' (Hamilton and Nestler 2019). This can have an impact on an individual's mental and physical health in a multitude of ways. Since the brain controls feelings, thinking, and behavior, drugs can significantly affect many areas of an individual's life. These include

keeping up with school or job tasks, maintaining employment due to inferior performance, affecting their aspirations and goals, and overall well-being.

2. **Impaired Cognitive Functions:** Prolonged drug use can affect important cognitive functions such as learning, memory, self-control, thinking, impulse control, and decision-making. The impairment can persist into adulthood even long after drug use has ceased (Mooney-Leber and Gould 2018, Volkow et al. 2016, Lyoo et al, 2006, Franklin et al., 2002). The substance user becomes unable to control their behavior and loses the ability to think clearly, leading to continued drug use and more poor decisions. This can cause poor academic achievement and negative consequences for relationships and future success overall. Drugs can cause teens to engage in risky behavior such as unprotected sex (increasing the risk for STIs or pregnancy), sharing drug paraphernalia, violence, criminal activity, health problems, driving under the influence, or work/school problems. These are only a few of the negative consequences but the list of harm is a long one.

3. **Psychiatric Disorders:** Drug use in teen years has been linked to increased risk of developing mental health disorders such as anxiety disorders, bipolar disorders, depression, personality disorders, attention-deficit hyperactivity disorder (ADHD) and schizophrenia (National Institute of Mental Health 2023). This can have a significant impact on their quality of life and well-being that can affect a person's

ability to work, and maintain relationships, lower quality of life, and impair functioning in everyday life.

4. **Increased Risk of Addiction:** Adolescent substance use dramatically increases the risk of developing a substance use disorder that can last a lifetime (Jordan and Andersen 2017). Because the teen brain is undergoing a maturation process or is still 'under construction,' it is very susceptible to damage caused by toxic chemicals. Imagine as if drugs actually 'trained' the teen brain to keep using it to seek pleasure and reward. Drugs become hardwired during the maturation process which can leave a lasting memory and trigger intense cravings throughout their life, long after abstinence.

Research in neuroscience has proven that drugs alter the dopaminergic reward system. The reward system is a network of brain regions involved in regulating pleasurable feelings and motivation. You can imagine this system as the brain's 'reward factory.' Drugs break into this 'reward factory' and change the functions, wiring, and structure of the 'equipment' (especially altering connections between neurons). Now the 'reward factory' only produces when drugs are consumed and they become lazy or nonresponsive to natural pleasurable experiences (i.e., spending time with friends, hobbies, etc.). The long-lasting changes in the brain are partly due to the release of massive amounts of dopamine (commonly referred to as the 'feel-good' neurotransmitter), which plays a critical role in regulating reward, pleasure, mood, and motivation in the brain. Our brain usually releases dopamine on its own when we engage in pleasurable activities and experiences such as eating our favorite food, having sex, and achieving goals. Drugs trigger the release of massive amounts of dopamine that the body can never produce on its own. Let me give you an example: What would you like more? A million dollars or a thousand dollars? Exactly. The brain gets flooded with the neurotransmitter dopamine with as much as ten times more than the natural release of these chemicals due to fun and pleasurable experiences (Di Chiara and Imperato,1988). The brain gets desensitized by getting used to the massive amounts of dopamine released and now requires a higher dose of a drug to create the same pleasurable effect as before. This is called 'tolerance.' This can lead to a cycle of repeated drug use that can cause changes in the brain while at the same time driving the path to addiction. Drug seeking becomes a top priority. In fact, the preferred substances become the only source of intense pleasure. Drugs literally wipe out all other pleasures for everyday activities that were perceived as fun before. More dopamine equals more pleasure, less dopamine equals less or even no pleasure.

1.2. Ticking Time Bomb: The Path to Addiction

Not everyone who uses drugs becomes addicted, but for many, it is a pathway to addiction. As you will later see in Chapter 3, several factors play a role in the development of an addiction, and it is different for everyone. But for everyone who becomes addicted to drugs, it always starts with the initial use. Many feel a sense of invincibility or believe that they 'for sure' will not ever get addicted. Nobody starts taking drugs to be miserable or wants to hurt themselves or their families. They do not wake up one day and decide "Today I want to start using drugs, become addicted, be homeless, end up in jail, etc.". It is a process that gradually takes over and spreads its toxicity to all areas of life. However, the reality is that addiction is pernicious, creeping in slowly and gradually over time. It progresses in severity as well. To illustrate this point better, let me break down the common stages and look at how addiction typically develops over time:

Stage1: Experimentation (First Time Use) => I Love It

It all starts with using it for the first time. An individual tries the drug to meet a certain need. Whether it is out of curiosity, to escape stress, or due to peer pressure. Drugs target the brain's reward system, and the release of dopamine will produce euphoric feelings. The individual will like it. And when people like something, they typically want to repeat the experience.

Stage 2: Occasional Use (Sometimes): I Like It

At this stage, the person may use the drug occasionally but not frequently. They still have control over their use and can quit or take a break at any time without withdrawal symptoms and/or intense cravings. The reason may be because they like it the first time because of other needs or reasons.

Regular Use (Often) => I Want It

The individual now uses drugs on a regular basis to seek the same effect as before. The brain remembers the rewarding behavior and wants to experience it again. The massive amounts of dopamine (neurotransmitters for pleasure and reward) the brain releases become less effective over time. The body develops **tolerance** and now requires more of the drug to achieve the same result.

Dependence (Always) => I Need It

With repeated use, people can develop a psychological and or physical dependence on the substance marked by intense cravings. When they develop a dependence on the substance and experience **withdrawal symptoms** if they do not take it. Withdrawal symptoms are the reaction of the body when it stops or significantly reduces the dose of a drug. They include such symptoms as nausea, vomiting, fever, muscle pain, seizures all the way to anxiety, depression, insomnia, or hallucinations. The symptoms depend on the type of substance, length of use, the dosage of the drug, and the person's own biology. People at this stage feel that they NEED it to a) feel normal again and b) to avoid withdrawal symptoms. Many do not even experience much pleasure at this point and only continue using the drug to feel 'normal' again without the hated withdrawal symptoms. Quitting on their own can be challenging at this point and proper intervention is needed for a successful recovery.

Drug Addiction => I Cannot Help it – I Have to Have it

At this point, the individual loses control and has the compulsive urge to use the drugs despite the negative consequences to self and others. To illustrate this better, imagine the loss of control as a broken brake on a car. Studies were able to prove the 'broken brake' due to drug use with the help of brain imaging. Researchers found out that drugs like cocaine, heroin, and methamphetamine, damaged the orbitofrontal cortex, an important brain region for decision-making and impulsivity (Everitt and Robbins 2013, Schoenbaum and Shaham 2008). And this means the following: Loss of control! It also shows why saying 'just stop' rarely works! And it also disproves the false narrative that addiction and relapse are the result of a character flaw, lack of motivation, and discipline. Drug use damages the brain and leaves permanent footprints. The brain remembers all drug-related cues. People, places, and things become primary triggers and cues for the preferred drug. The smell of the substance (i.e., tobacco), the sight of drug paraphernalia (i.e., pipe, syringe) and the setting (i.e., preferred location for drug use) can all trigger intense cravings. Just the thought alone can become a cue and reminder of the positive feeling and trigger cravings for the drug!

1.3. What is an Addiction Anyway?

I would like to give you the proper definition of addiction and the criteria that are used to diagnose it. This will help you better understand what your loved one is going through and also recognize the warning signs and symptoms of addiction. Having a clear understanding of the behavior and symptoms of addiction can also help you identify the seriousness of the problem with drug use. Moreover, when seeking professional help with urgency. You will be better prepared to provide detailed information to professionals that can lead to more accurate diagnoses and an effective treatment plan. The proper definition of drug addiction, also known as substance use disorder (SUD), is a chronic, relapsing disorder characterized by compulsive drug seeking and use despite harmful consequences (National Institute on Drug Abuse 2020).

The Diagnostic and Statistical Manual of Mental Disorders (DSM) is a manual currently in its 5th Revision, used by healthcare professionals to diagnose mental health conditions, including substance use disorder. For an individual to be diagnosed with SUD, they need to meet certain criteria. At least two of the following 11 criteria need to be met within a 12-month period to receive this diagnosis (Hasin et al., 2013):

1. **Impaired Control:** Substance is taken in <u>larger amounts</u> or for longer periods of time than intended.

2. **Unable to Cut Down:** <u>Unable to cut back</u> or control substance use.

3. **Time and Effort:** Much <u>time is spent</u> to obtain, use and recover from the effects of the substance.

4. **Craving and Desire:** <u>Strong desire</u> and craving to use the substance.

5. **Failure to Meet Obligations:** <u>Failure</u> to fulfill major obligations at work, school, home, etc.

6. **Give up or Reduce Important Activities:** Social, occupational, or recreational <u>activities may be given up or reduced</u> because of substance use (i.e., hobbies, social gatherings)

7. **Use Despite Social or Interpersonal Problems:** Substance use is continued <u>despite social and interpersonal consequences</u> (i.e., relationship or social life)

8. **Risky Use:** The individual may <u>use drugs in risky situations</u>, for example, driving under the influence or having unprotected sex.

9. **Tolerance:** The substance user may develop <u>tolerance</u> (needing a higher dose for the same effect)

10. **Withdrawals:** Experiences <u>withdrawal symptoms</u> when trying to cut back or quit.

11. **Continued Use Despite Negative Consequences:** Use despite adverse <u>physical or psychological consequences</u>.

The DSM-5 classifies the severity of the disorder that ranges from mild to severe depending on the number of criteria met. Meeting 2-3 criteria are considered as mild, 4-5 as moderate, and 6 or more is classified as severe. These criteria are for your information only and not to diagnose or evaluate your teen on your own. Substance use disorder is a complex condition. A comprehensive assessment by a qualified and trained healthcare professional is necessary to accurately diagnose and evaluate the physical and mental health conditions of your child.

1.4. Why Drug Addiction is a Brain Disease

Many people wrongfully believe that addiction is simply a matter of moral weakness or lack of willpower. But in reality, it is a brain disease, and the scientific community has proven this fact. Research shows that drug addiction is a chronic, relapsing medical brain disease because of its similar features to common medical diseases such as diabetes, cardiovascular disease, or cancer (Volkow et al. 2016, Volkow and Koob 2015). They can all cause premature death, carry the risk of relapse even long after recovery, and can improve or worsen with good or bad habits. In addition, individuals can carry a genetic vulnerability making them prone to develop those diseases (more on genetic vulnerability in the next chapter). This fact is hard to grasp for many because drug use starts with voluntary use (control) and with making their own decisions. What people do not realize is the fact that drug use changes the function and structure of the brain which affects a person's behavior, decision-making, and ability to control their drug use. It also creates powerful urges and cravings (no control) even when they are aware of the negative consequences and moreover, even if they no longer experience pleasure from using the drug. Compulsive drug-seeking behavior is a hallmark of addiction and one of the reasons why individuals with a drug addiction cannot just quit because they are told so. This is true even if they want to quit. Wishful thinking has never cured heart disease or cancer and it will not cure drug addiction either. Some people can quit drug use on their own without professional treatment with strong willpower, however, this is not the case for everyone. Recognizing addiction as a brain disease does not mean that we excuse their behavior and choices. Holding them accountable can encourage them to take responsibility for their actions and help them find the courage to seek recovery. We also need to encourage them to seek help by making it clear that drug addiction is treatable, and that recovery is possible. Many have walked the path to recovery before. Sharing the success stories of others can further empower them and provide hope as an added motivator for individuals to take the necessary steps toward their own recovery and healing.

1.5. The Healing Power of the Brain

Our brain is an incredibly powerful organ. It has remarkable healing abilities that make it possible to constantly change and adapt to the environment; a phenomenon that is called 'neuroplasticity'. With new experiences and behaviors, the brain can form new neural connections and pathways. Because of the brain's ability to rewire and reorganize itself throughout life, it can also heal and reverse <u>some of the damage</u> inflicted by the drug once drug use has ceased (Garavan et al., 2013). With the cessation of drug use and an engagement in a healthy and positive lifestyle, the brain will adapt and significantly improve. This is great news for all those who think that the damage is irreversible and thus were giving up hope for a successful healing. This is also news that makes sense. Just as our bodies have the ability to heal from an illness and injury, so can our brain as well. But be aware that I underlined some of the damage because some is simply permanent. Especially when drug use has begun during adolescence when the brain is still developing. It can leave irreparable neurological damage. It is therefore urgent to course correct the destructive behavior to reduce the risk of long-term consequences. That recovery and healing is possible does not need to be proved by brain science. Just knowing that millions of people have walked the path to recovery is proof that it is possible to heal with the right support and resources. It is estimated that ten percent of all adults in the United States have had a drug use disorder, according to Addiction Help.com in March 2023. Let us turn our attention to the root causes of addiction to shed light into why bright young kids take such a huge risk and put their health and future into jeopardy.

A mother's love;

always flowing and

never bending.

Chapter Two

HIDDEN DANGERS AND FALSE PROMISES OF DRUGS

2.1. Lying Chemicals: The Deceptive Nature of Drugs

In this chapter we explore and unravel the deceptive nature of drugs. While drugs provide an artificial sense of euphoric happiness and pleasure in an instant, the chemically induced happy feelings come at a significant cost. What is though are the negative effects and consequences for individuals and their families. It makes users view life through a rose-tinted lens that blocks out reality and blinds them to its harmful effects. Due to their distorted perception of the world, they overlook or ignore potential harm to their physical and mental health. Ironically, while many consume drugs to ease their emotional and physical pain by changing their current state, they are causing even more pain and more suffering. Problems do not just magically disappear; they are actually getting a whole lot worse.

Drug use can result in double isolation: First, drug use interferes with social activities and leaves less time (or even no time) with loved ones, it can lead to increased isolation and loneliness. Secondly, other people distance themselves due to the stigma and shame or concern for their own safety. The loneliness and increased isolation cause emotional pain, yet it is another reason to use drugs to numb the negative emotions. Besides losing touch with loved ones, feeding the beast will grow the problem and make it spill over to all areas of life. It strains relationships with friends and family, causes problems in school or work, leads to financial problems, and affects their overall quality of life and health. Personal goals that used to be exciting now no longer matter. The pleasant and joyful things become overshadowed. Artificial pleasure destroys and replaces real pleasure. For the purpose of uncovering the misleading and harmful effects of the artificial experience, allow me for a moment, to compare drugs with a few negative words and look up their definition in the online Marriam-Webster (2023). Their shared characteristics will shed light on the true nature of drugs and may serve as a revelation for many:

> **Drugs:** Imitation of real pleasure that feels natural and original but is not
>
> **Counterfeit:** "Made in imitation of something else but intent to deceive"
>
> **Drugs:** Can lead to distorted perception of problems, reality, and the world.
>
> **Unreal:** "Lacking in reality, substance, or genuineness"
>
> **Drugs:** Make people believe that they found the secret to a lasting happiness and lets them think they can control their situation
>
> **Deception:** "Act of causing someone to accept as true or valid what is false or invalid"

Drugs: The emotions and feelings caused by drugs are not based on authentic experience and are therefore not true, real, or genuine.

Fake "Not true, real or genuine"

Do you see the commonalities? You can look up similar synonyms like fakery, fraud, misleading, false, untrue, inaccurate or untrue and I think we can agree that you will find common characteristics to drugs. I find it helpful to build an association between those negative words and drugs. This realization has created several "aha-moments" and caused a shift in perspective with my clients. I call this an effective strategy that can lead to a wake-up call because it shows what drugs really are and what they represent. It is an invitation to let go of the fake and instead, hold on to the authentic way of living. We need to teach young minds that life can be tough, and adversity is inevitable. We must encourage authenticity and true experiences of all emotions, whether they be good or bad. It is important to recognize and teach our children that true happiness is an internal job. It comes from within. We are the gatekeepers of our emotions and feelings and if we do not allow external factors to disturb our internal peace, there simply will not be any need for artificial support for happiness. Real happiness cannot be injected, snorted or inhaled. Real happiness hides in activities that make us lose time, happiness creeps in when we view life as a gift rather than taking it for granted. Real happiness occurs when we change goals and dreams that make us grow as a human, when we foster healthy relationships and enjoy others' company and when we give as much back to society as we get. This is not only true of happiness but also true of fulfillment. I hope that you will pass on this outlook on life to your family so they too can embrace nature and reality with open arms.

2.2. Debunking Hidden Dangers of Legal Drugs

Legal drugs are substances that are permitted by law that can be purchased or prescribed by a licensed health care provider. They can be easily purchased in pharmacies, convenience stores, gas stations, and supermarkets. There is a common misconception that legal drugs are somehow less harmful or perhaps that they are even good for you. Because they are legal, they are socially acceptable, and many are well-advertised, giving the false impression to the public that they are safe to use. However, they also have side effects that can cause harm to your health and body. Let us look at some examples of legal substances and debunk their hidden dangers. Please note that each one of these legal substances has numerous side effects and too many to list in this section. I will therefore highlight a few to make you aware that legally does indeed not mean harmless:

Alcohol: According to the National Institute on Alcohol Abuse and Alcoholism, there are about ninety-five thousand alcohol related deaths each year, making it the third leading cause of accidental deaths in the United States. (NIAAA 2023). That is nearly 11 deaths every hour. The Centers for Disease Control and Prevention has listed a range of risks and consequences for teen alcohol use including disruption of normal growth and brain development, increased risk of suicide and homicide, violence, accidents as well as skipping school (2022). Yes, alcohol is a legal as well as culturally a very popular drug. However, its legality does not eliminate its risks to your health and quality of life. A group of researchers compared alcohol and heroin dependence and concluded that alcohol is in fact more dangerous than heroin regarding physical, social and financial terms" (Lee at al., 2011).

Nicotine: You might think, 'well that is the least harmful of all substances." But you would be mistaken. There are too many side effects of nicotine use to mention every single one, but I want to briefly highlight just a few. Smokers are twenty times more likely to develop lung cancer and reduce their life expectancy by ten years (Mons et al., 2018, Doll et al., 2004). There is evidence that consuming nicotine for just seven days enhances the rewarding effects of cocaine in the brain (Kandel & Kandel 2014). Researchers go as far as claiming that nicotine serves as a gateway drug to cocaine and marijuana because nicotine primes the brain for the rewarding properties of those substances. Smoking is also linked to increased risk of developing dementia and cognitive decline (Anstey et al., 2007). E-cigarettes have gained such popularity among teens that I find it important to highlight their dangers. They are not only highly addictive but also contain the type of nicotine that is among the most addictive. Just like regular cigarettes, they too can cause cancer, and even those that are labeled as 'nicotine-free', studies have found that they still do (Shmerling 2019, El-Hellani et al., 2015). As you can imagine from the risks mentioned, nicotine use in the early years can have a significant negative effect on the brain. Using nicotine during adolescence increases the risk of developing mental and cognitive issues later in life (Goriounova and Mansvelder 2023).

Marijuana: Reality: Marijuana is an addictive substance and harmful to physical, mental, and brain health, especially when the use started in the teen years. As you will recall from Chapter 1, the teen brain is not fully developed and is still changing in structure. Marijuana can intervene in the normal development of the brain affecting important cognitive functions (Camchong et al., 2016). It can also trigger mental illnesses such as anxiety, depression as well as suicidal thoughts. But that is not all. Teens who consume marijuana and later develop marijuana use disorder lost an average of eight IQ points between the ages of 18 to 38. Even worse, these points do not come back when they quit using either (National Institute on Drug Abuse 2019, Meier 2012). Another reason many thinks marijuana is safe to use is there is something called 'medical marijuana' that is used as a treatment for patients suffering from various diseases such as epilepsy or cancer. They justify their consumption by thinking that it cannot be bad for you since it is used as part of treatment. But what they do not realize is that medical marijuana is stripped from its intoxicating properties and has little to no THC (tetrahydrocannabinol), the chemical that is responsible for the euphoric mood.

Over-the-Counter Medications: Over-the-counter (OTC) medications can often be thought of and perceived as harmless as hardly anybody reads the fine print on the label for proper dosing instructions and risk factors. The truth is that they can have risks and side effects just like prescription drugs do. For example, taking OTC medications for too long and in excessive dosage can have serious health consequences. Ibuprofen and Paracetamol, for example, can lead to high blood pressure and gastrointestinal bleeding with prolonged use (Ngo und Bajaj 2020, McCrae et al., 2018). Another example is laxatives that many conveniently use to help with constipation. They can decrease bowel functioning and cause dependency with overuse (Mayo Clinic 2022). I compare over-the-counter medication to guns. They can be used for good or evil. A gun may save your life or kill you. Wal-Mart or Dicks Sporting Goods have whole department shelves full of different sizes and models. Does that make them any less lethal?

Prescription Medication: Prescription medication can be safe to use if taken properly and as directed. It is important to note that just because a doctor prescribed the medication does not mean that it is safe. Quite the contrary, they are prescription painkillers (or opioids like Oxycontin, Fentanyl, Vicodin), for a reason! Because it is not safe for people to buy them over the counter. Some prescription medications work just like illegal narcotics because of similar chemical properties. It is not uncommon for people to continue using narcotic painkillers long after their initial reason for starting them has ended. Taking them for an extended period can lead to dependence and can often lead users to transition to illegal drugs such as heroin. In fact, 75% of heroin users started off by using prescription opioids and later turned to heroin because of the cost, because heroin is cheaper (Get Smart About Drugs (2021). It should only be used for its intended purpose, to treat a specific medical condition and as prescribed by your healthcare professional. Using prescription medication for recreational use is not only dangerous but can also cause serious life-threatening consequences like overdose and cardiac arrest (Sakhuja et al., 2017).

2.3. Myth Busting Facts about Drugs

It is time to eliminate some familiar myths and false beliefs about some common drugs and replace these myths with the facts. Many people believe in myths because they simply do not know the actual facts. Thus, they have limited knowledge and must rely on popular culture, rumors or even hearsay to form their opinion. With all the information out there, it gets difficult to separate what is fact from fiction. This is extremely dangerous. Lack of knowledge can lead to underestimating the effects and risks associated with the body and mind. In fact, in my interviews with hundreds of substance users, I have yet to meet one who knew the science behind how drugs actually work. The pharmaceutical industry, media and popular culture are not great sources for getting accurate information. In fact, it is actually the opposite. They promote myths about certain drugs to further their own agendas. Have you ever noticed how fast they disclose the risks and side effects on commercials when advertising for a certain drug? It is almost as if it is not important if they say it so fast. It is because they do not want you to pay close attention to it and scare you. They want you to buy it and not be scared. The existence of myths about drugs highlights how important it is to educate people on the risks and science behind drugs. By dispelling myths and exposing the facts, we can help make informed decisions about their drug use. By breaking down some myths about drugs, we can also help eliminate stigmatization, discrimination, and negative attitudes against people who use drugs (more on stigmatization in Chapter 8.5.). Here are a few myths I would like to discuss:

Myth No. 1
Only Weak People Who Lack Willpower Use Drugs

Reality: This may be the dumbest but all too common misconception about drugs that is circulating out there. Anybody from all walks of life and from any socioeconomic status from college students, athletes, to CEO's can struggle with addiction and nobody is immune to its harmful effects. Addiction is a complex disease. While willpower can be an important factor in resisting drug use, it is not the only one. As discussed in the previous chapter, it can also involve biological and environmental factors and many who use drugs face challenges and issues that have nothing to do with willpower. Stigmatizing and shaming people as lacking willpower is counterproductive and only prevents them further from seeking the help they need. Addiction is a medical condition and can affect anyone regardless of willpower, strength of character or moral values.

Myth No.2

People Who Use Drugs are Criminals, Bad and Dangerous

Reality: People who use drugs are not criminals, bad, or dangerous people. Many who use drugs are not involved in criminal activities and are, in fact, productive members of our society. Because the possession of illegal drugs is against the law, it becomes easy for many to get involved in drug-related offenses, when in fact, the underlying issue is the addiction. Jails and prisons are full of individuals with drug-related criminal records. It would be like locking down people who have type 2 diabetes because they did not take care of their bodies. Yes, type 2 diabetes is a preventable disease and is primarily self-inflicted due to poor lifestyle choices (Uusitupa et al., 2019). To be clear, I am not excusing or promoting drug use. But I am advocating for easy access to healthcare and support to overcome their addiction regardless of how their addiction began. It can improve the health and well-being of the individual, but also help them become productive members of their communities while at the same time reducing the burden on taxpayers.

Myth No. 3
Anybody Could Quit if They Really Wanted

Reality: As discussed previously, drugs can cause changes in brain chemistry and functions that can reduce a person's ability to control their drug use, think clearly and make rational decisions. It can impair their ability in decision-making and self-control. It therefore is challenging for them to quit on their own. We also discussed that addiction can be caused by several factors such as genetics and mental health conditions that are outside an individual's control. For a successful recovery, people also need to learn new skills such as breaking bad habits, controlling cravings, and learning better and healthier ways to deal with negative emotions. These are all important tools they must learn from skilled professionals to successfully overcome their addiction.

Myth No. 4
The Damage Caused by Using Drugs is Irreversible

Reality: Some of the damage caused by drug use is reversible. Of course, this depends on several factors such as the type of drug used, the duration of use as well as the intensity of use. However, research suggests that some of the changes caused by drugs can be reversed with treatment and cessation of drug use. Thanks to neuroplasticity, the brain has a tremendous power to constantly change and adapt to current lifestyle choices. For example, research has shown that people who abstained from cocaine use for one year had cognitive functioning like those who never used cocaine, which shows that memory and attention can improve (Vonmoos et al., 2014). Even liver damage caused by alcohol use can be repaired if users stop drinking (Thomes et al., 2021). Damage to the heart caused by methamphetamines could also be reversed with abstinence and medical treatment (American College of Cardiology 2021). I often hear people use excuses such as 'I have used it so long; the damage is already done. There is no point in stopping now'. I do not accept their excuses, but unfortunately, they do. How can they make an informed decision if they do not know the facts? Please note that I said 'some of the damage' at the beginning of the paragraph which means that not all the damage can be cured. Unfortunately, some of the damage will in fact be permanent. The best way to avoid any kind of damage to the brain and body is not to use drugs in the first place or at least reduce the frequency of drug use. Please use any opportunity you get to share these facts with your family.

Myth No. 5
Only Poor People Use Drugs:

Reality: Drug addiction can affect anybody from all socioeconomic statuses and from all walks of life. As discussed in Chapter 3, drug addiction can be the cause of many factors. Genetics, environment, and mental health conditions do not care how much money people have in their bank accounts. The misconception is usually based on media portrayal and of witnessing people on the streets who are easy to identify as drug users. People on the streets are on the streets because they have nowhere else to go. They do not see the people doing drugs in the comfort of their own homes. I have met so many people addicted to drugs that you would never be able to tell just by looking at them. I have done an internship at a consumption center (DCC) in Germany and watched hundreds of people walk in and take drugs. DCC is a supervised healthcare facility where individuals can consume drugs in a safe environment. I have witnessed a man with missing limbs crawling into the facility to take his shot and I have seen a young man in a business suit come in for his dose. I have witnessed that drug use can affect anyone and that no one is immune to its harmful effects. Not even the wealthy. Just think of celebrities like Michael Jackson, Whitney Houston, Marilyn Monroe, and Prince who we lost to drugs, and they are just a few examples. Celebrity magazines are full of examples that drug addiction has no social class preference and therefore does not care about the size of your bank account. We all have the same brain, and our brain and bodies function the same way. Drugs are harmful to everyone and can kill anyone.

Myth No. 6
Trying Drugs Just One Time Will Not Cause Addiction

Reality: While it is true that not everyone who uses drugs become addicted, the idea that using drugs just once is safe is an extremely dangerous myth. This can lead many to a false sense of security and confidence to experiment with drugs even more so. Even ONE single use can prime the brain to crave more. Researchers have found that after one single dose of cocaine or amphetamine can make changes in the brain that could increase the risk of developing addiction (Runegaard et al., 2019). Another study discovered that after trying cocaine for the first time, the feeling of 'wanting' and 'liking' the drug were significant predictors of becoming dependent and using it for a lifetime (Lambert et al., 2006). While not everyone who uses drugs become addicted, everyone who are addicted started with the initial use. The experience will be perceived as pleasurable and fun, and this motivates many to do it again and again. Leading many down the rabbit hole of addiction when occasional use spirals to regular use and then to dependence. It is important to recognize and pass on to our loved ones that there is absolutely no safe amount of drugs and not using them is the best way to avoid any possible risks and consequences and stay healthy.

Myth No. 7
Using Drugs Responsibly is Safe and is Not Addictive

All drugs have the potential for serious harm and even responsible use can carry significant risk. Drugs can impair judgment and decisions as they can alter thoughts, feelings, and behaviors. While it could be safe for adults to occasionally enjoy a glass of wine, it is not safe to drive. Even tiny amounts of alcohol, for example 0.015% BAC (blood alcohol concentration) which is way below the legal driving limit of 0.08% can dramatically impair hand-eye coordination, according to recent research finding (Tyson et al... 2020). How about smoking just one cigarette a day? Well, this is not a good idea. According to research findings, smoking just one cigarette a day increases the risk for heart disease and stroke by 48%-74% (Johnson 2018). If legal drugs can cause this much harm, you can only imagine what illegal drugs are capable of doing. Any substance has side effects and can cause serious harm and education on the potential risks is important to making informed decisions to minimize risks.

Educating yourself about the myths and facts of addiction and the drugs your child is using is an important first step to avoid and to address drug use by your loved ones. There are massive amounts of information and resources from online platforms, books, to healthcare professionals. Write down all your questions and look for answers until you find them. Nobody will ever care about you and your family's health as much as you do. To make an informed decision, always seek reliable and accurate information from trusted sources and educate your children to do the same.

2.4. Identifying Underlying Needs and Emotions

While the reason is different for everybody, sometimes people use drugs for excitement, pleasure, peer pressure, to connect with others or simply out of curiosity or boredom. And for others, it serves as self-medication to cope with emotional and psychological issues such as depression, stress, or anxiety. People often turn to drugs to fulfill certain desires and need a substitute for something that is missing in their lives. Only by finding those unmet needs can we help address those appropriately, in healthier and more effective ways. In order to truly address substance use in your child, we need to understand their underlying needs to find out the motivation behind their substance use. It is not always easy to find the motivation for drug use. Sometimes we can be blind to their needs because we assume that their beliefs, expectations, and needs are the same as ours. Or we do not take the time to find out what it is that they need for their happiness and well-being. While the motivation for drug use is different for everybody, quite often it is driven by the **hedonistic principle** (also called the pleasure-pain principle). It is the idea that humans are driven primarily to experience pleasure and to avoid pain. In both cases, the goal in both is either to enhance the well-being or restore it. Sadly, drugs can satisfy both. It can provide short-term pleasure and euphoria and also help alleviate pain and discomfort. This can start a vicious cycle when people desire to repeat the experience of pleasure or avoid the pain and discomfort of withdrawal symptoms. The short-term immediate effect leads to long-term and potentially lasting consequences. To help your child avoid those long-term consequences and pain, you need to find out what caused the drug use in the first place. This is important because by finding out the root cause, void, or need, we can accomplish the following:

a. You can address the root cause of the problem instead of treating the symptom.

b. Treatment providers can tailor their treatment plan according to the specific needs of a patient. This can help the treatment to be more effective and can reduce the risk of relapse.

c. You can help your child find healthier alternatives to meet those needs.

d. You can take proactive measures to help your child with proper intervention such as counseling and education.

e. Sometimes parents blame themselves when something goes wrong with their child. Knowing the underlying need can help relieve those feelings of guilt.

f. By knowing your child's needs, you can better communicate and empathize with your child which could significantly improve the quality of your communication and relationship with your child.

To explore potential causes, the following questions can help you think deeper to help discover what part of your child's life could be in imbalance. What is he or she lacking or trying to restore? These questions are inspired by Keith J. Cunningham, a successful entrepreneur and business coach. His book 'The Road Less Stupid: Advice from the Chairman of the Board' (2018). I learned the value of deliberately carving out 'thinking time'. While he uses thinking time for his business, what a difference it is to make time to think about your loved one's well-being? In my opinion, business is worthless when your child is suffering or struggling with a big problem. So, lets now look at a few questions that can help you THINK about what it can be that is causing your child to engage in substance use:

- What purpose or unmet need is he/she trying to meet?
- To what problem is he/she trying to find a solution?
- What value could he/she be trying to get from drugs?
- How would I evaluate my child's current level of self-esteem/self-worth?
- Does my child have positive relationships/role models/mentors?
- Is my child struggling with a mental health disorder?
- What was my child complaining about recently? What was bothering him/her?
- Is my child possibly trying to fit into a peer group? Who could be a bad influence?
- Do I spend enough quality time with my child? What can I do to bring us closer?
- What is the quality of my relationship with my child?
- Did I educate my child about the risks associated with drug use?
- Is my child getting enough love and attention?
- Are drugs easily accessible at home/environment?
- Did I model responsible behavior around drugs?
- Could it be that my child is bored / lacking excitement?
- Did my child experience any adverse / stressful / traumatic event recently?
- Were there any recent changes in the environment that could have triggered it?

How do you think your child would answer the above questions based on their personality, experiences, history and current state? What is positive for you may not be positive for your child. If you think you or another family member is the source of pain, abuse, or chaos in your child's life, get professional help immediately. By addressing underlying problems, the treatment provider can help work with the whole family as a unit. This will help to strengthen the relationships between family members, improve the mood and well- being of everyone, help new and effective ways to communicate better and teach how to overcome problems and adversities. This self-soothing and temporary relief and comfort comes at a big cost. For many who experienced such horrific and traumatic events, the emotional pain can be so severe, that they think the only way to tolerate and cope with it is through using drugs. Your knowledge and understanding can be a valuable tool to educate and empower your teen to make healthy choices and take proactive steps toward recovery.

Tenderness, protectiveness,

and selflessness

– A Mom

Chapter Three

POWER OF GENETICS AND ENVIRONMENT

3.1. The Link Between Mental Health and Substance Use

There is a strong link between mental health and substance use. The scientific community has provided numerous studies that show that mental health disorders often co-occur with addiction. The coexistence of both mental health conditions and substance use disorder is known as **co-occurring disorder.** People who suffer from mental health disorders are twice as likely as people in the general population to develop a substance use disorder (Silverman et al., 2016). Many people with mental health problems may turn to drugs to self-medicate or to numb their symptoms. Yet others develop mental health issues because of their substance use. Drugs can also worsen an existing mental health problem or cause the development of a totally new mental health issue. A number of mental health problems can emerge due to the use of drugs. For example, there seems to be a particularly strong correlation between PTSD and substance use disorder. Studies show that about 59% of young adults with PTSD struggle with substance abuse problems (The National Child Traumatic Stress Network 2008). An investigation of opioid-related death cases showed that the deceased were eight times more likely to suffer from schizophrenia (Watkins et al., 2019). Other common mental health problems that often co-occur with substance use are antisocial personality disorder, borderline depression, and anxiety disorders (Kelly and Daley 2013). It is also possible that common risk factors for substance use, and mental health can trigger the emergence of both disorders at the same time (Santucci 2012). A comprehensive approach is very important that addresses both mental health and addiction simultaneously for a successful and long-term recovery. For example, if anxiety and depression issues are not addressed during the addiction treatment, people are at high risk of relapse as they could reach for drugs in the hopes of alleviating their symptoms.

3.2. The Role of Genes in the World of Drugs

Vulnerabilities can echo through many generations and families. Drug addiction, though, looks like a personal choice on the surface because of voluntary initiation, but in fact it can be a product of our ancestors and thus play a role in the development of substance use disorder. Research confirms that substance use disorder is highly heritable. If an individual has a family member who is addicted to drugs, that increases their own likelihood to develop an addiction to drugs. It is estimated that the heritability of addiction can range from 39% to 72% (Goldberg and Gould 2019). Adoption studies have provided strong evidence that addiction is highly heritable. When biological parents used drugs, it significantly increased the risk for the adopted offspring to use drugs as well (Kendler et al.,

2012). The reason could be **epigenetic changes**. Substance use by mom and dad can be passed on to the fetus as drugs alter their genes that pass on to their unborn child. This significantly increases the risk for the offspring to develop substance use disorder themselves and makes them vulnerable to all kinds of problems such as deficits in cognitive functions and accelerated aging (Goldberg and Gould 2019, Wanner et al., 2019). Simply put, previous generations can pass on the vulnerability to the next generation. Please note that genetic predisposition alone does not determine the development of an addiction. Some people may have a genetic predisposition that may only manifest with exposure to certain environmental factors such as stress, trauma, exposure to drugs, etc. The genes may never get expressed, similar to a light switch that remains turned off.

3.3. Environmental Factors Leading to Using Drug

The environment where someone grows up in is crucially important. The environment your child spends time in will influence their behavior and decisions. An individual's upbringing, social circle, and experiences can all affect the likelihood of developing this disorder if it is toxic. I see college students who have never had a habit of drinking now drink alcohol on a regular basis just because it is part of the college culture. It is almost expected of people to drink when they join a gathering or a party. Since we all have a high need to be accepted and belong to a group, the pressure is high to conform to the expectations of the environment.

Children learn a lot by observing and imitating adult behavior. Based on my observation with incarcerated women in jails, I can only confirm this. Habits and behaviors seem to run in families. I have seen cases where multiple family members were incarcerated at the same time. This is not a coincidence. This is **'social learning'** at its core. Social learning is a theory that explains how people learn by observing and imitating others rather than through direct experience and reinforcement. For example, when children watch how their parents cope with stress and other problems by using substances, they are likely to model this coping mechanism when they are stressed themselves.

Environmental Factors That Can Contribute to Drug Use

There are several environmental factors that can contribute to drug use. See this chapter as an introduction for the chapters to follow where we will go into more detail on the influence of different environmental factors like friends, mentors, and the impact of primary care giver.

- **Friends**: Who are the people in your child's immediate environment? What kind of people come and go to your house? Are they known for criminal activity or drug use? If yes, take immediate action! (Please refer to Chapter 5.4. to learn more about the influence of negative friendships).

- **Safe and Stable Home Environment**: Unstable, toxic, problematic, and stressful family environment are risk factors for alcohol and drug use. Home should always be a safe haven for children, not a battle ground. There is evidence that children growing up in an environment with alcohol use, molestation, criminal activity, lack of parental care, and lack of a healthy relationship to parents were more vulnerable to drug use (Zimić and Jukić, 2012). If you have identified an area of concern, take immediate steps to address it.

- **Easy Access to Drugs:** Having substances readily available in the environment just makes it easier and more likely for teens to use drugs. They get encouraged to use drugs when their environment gives them the impression that it is normal and simply part of life. Location of school, neighborhood, and community all play an important role. If drugs are easily accessible and available in the immediate environment, this can influence and shape their life.

- **Parents Social Environment**: What about your friends? What kind of people are you or your partner exposing your children? These include friends and family who could be excellent role models to thrive or excellent models for drug use. You may be leading by example, but your social circle needs to be aligned with your values as well (more on leading by example in Chapter 4). Prioritize your child's safety and well-being and be vigilant to what kind of people to whom you expose your family.

Environmental factors are so powerful that they can even change our gene expression. Some genes can be just like a light switch turned on or off depending on lifestyle choice and experiences (Pelletir 2018, Pinel et al., 2018). Because the teenage brain undergoes significant changes, the right environment can promote healthy brain development and function. Be intentional about exposing your child to a positive environment for them to grow and learn and become their best. By equipping them with the right resources in the right environment, we can help mold their lives for success during adolescence and beyond.

As we have discussed in this chapter, drugs harm the brain and body in a multitude of ways, affecting health, quality of life, and well-being. It is nearly impossible to pinpoint a single cause as a trigger as it is usually an interplay between several factors. The risk of developing an addiction increases the more vulnerabilities a person is carrying. And having a vulnerability does not necessarily mean that it will lead to addiction. For example, a genetic vulnerability to addiction can be overpowered by a resilient environment with no environmental triggers and vice versa. Being in a very stressful environment can make people become addicted to drugs even though they do not carry any genetic vulnerability. Addiction is a complex problem and both nature and nurture have a significant impact on an individual. Both need to be considered in trying to understand drug addiction.

3.4. How Personal Factors Can Shape Addiction

There is no single trait that can predict with certainty any addictive behavior. However, there are certain personal factors that can increase the risk of addiction among those are impulsivity, sensation-seeking, and hopelessness (González Ponce et al., 2019). Impulsivity for example, can lead to engaging in risky behavior such as experimenting with drugs or alcohol without thinking through their risks and consequences. Also, sensation seekers may use drugs just for the thrill of it. Let us not forget the person's own temperament and natural tendencies toward certain emotions, behavior, and reactions. Some individuals who are more resilient, are good at regulating their mood and emotions, and minor challenges do not seem to bother them. But there are others, who are hypersensitive, easy to persuade, and can get knocked off easily by minor stressful events. In both cases their reaction to adversity and outside forces will be different. We also need to consider an individual's own biological makeup because an abnormal brain structure can favor the use of drugs. For example, researchers have found that a small Orbitofrontal Cortex (important brain region for impulsivity and decision-making) at age 12 could predict cannabis use at age 16 (Cheetham et al., 2012). Yet another study found structural abnormalities in different brain regions of people with a drug addiction (Ersche et al.,.2012). You might be thinking that those changes were the result of drug use, but they were not. It seems as if they were present at birth since their biological siblings of the test subjects also have those same abnormalities, but who were not using drugs. Two siblings – same abnormal brain structure – different outcomes. How come? This only highlights one more time how important it is to look at the whole picture and consider the other risk factors like genes, environment, individual personality, and the mindset about drugs.

3.5. Horrors of Adverse Childhood Experiences

The power of the environment can have a profound impact on a person's physical, emotional, and mental health. Especially early experiences shapes who we become. There is a growing body of research that shows that adverse childhood experiences (ACEs) can have long-lasting effects on an individual's development. Research has shown that the root cause of addiction can be traced back all the way to negative childhood experiences (Felitti 2003). As discussed in Chapter 1, the brain is malleable and undergoing rapid growth. ACEs such as abuse and neglect can significantly impair the healthy development of their neurocircuits laying the foundation for lifelong mental and physical effects. In fact, childhood neglect has such a detrimental effect to a healthy development of the brain that kids who are exposed to severe neglect have 'significantly' smaller brains than normal newborns (Perry 2002). ACEs mold the brain permanently. Any kind of maltreatment, emotional, physical, or verbal abuse can have serious consequences for a lot of problems and that includes addiction. Nakazawa (2015) is making a valid point by saying that 'biography becomes your biology'. Adverse childhood experiences (ACEs) are more common than one might think. A shocking 60% of adults have experienced at least one ACE, 40% two ACEs, and 15% of adults have experienced at least four or more. People who experienced four or more ACEs face:

- 1000% higher risk to engage in intravenous drug use.
- 1220% higher risk of suicide.
- 460% higher risk to suffer from depression.
- 430% higher risk to abuse alcohol.

The list goes on with multiple elevated health risks from heart disease, cancer, obesity, diabetes, and asthma, all the way to changes in brain structure. Experiences leave clues. When life gets stressful and overwhelming, it is easy to become preoccupied with our own problems, issues, and even trauma from our past. I see it time and time again that children suffer at the hands of their parents own unresolved issues from their past. These unresolved issues can have bitter consequences. I have witnessed this with my clients. I always stress the importance of resolving past trauma and emotional garbage as soon as possible, ideally before having children. If you do not want your children to suffer from the effects of your unresolved issues and trauma, please get help. If you do not get the help you need for your emotional and psychological well-being, your children might need help at some point in their lives because you did not. It all starts with us. When we are strong, we can raise strong, resilient children.

Unbreakable

Unshakable

Unconditional.

Chapter Four

LEADING BY EXAMPLE

4.1. Why Being a Good Role Model is Important

If you are the primary care giver to your children, you play a critical role in your child's life and are the most influential person. You can help shape your child's world for the better through your actions. Your attitudes, beliefs, and behavior serve as a role model and blueprint for their own. Children do not always do what they are told to do. They do what parents do. They learn by watching and imitating. It is like the case of obesity. If parents are obese due to unhealthy eating habits, so is the child. The child eats what the parents cook. The same is true for drugs or other harmful behaviors. The child consumes and absorbs mentally and emotionally what is happening in front of them, in their immediate environment. That is why it is important to demonstrate the behaviors and attitudes that you want to see in your children. The foundation of substance use prevention starts with providing a secure, stable, and safe home environment for your children to thrive. Just like the foundation of a house, you cannot build a strong house without the most basic structure that forms the foundation. It is the foundation upon which we build their sense of self. To raise happy, resilient, and confident children they need supportive and attentive parents who love and nurture their offspring. Most importantly, they need love and connection. We all do. We are social creatures. We all need a sense of belonging, purpose, and security. We are wired to bond and connect with others. In fact, it is so important, that it is crucial for our very survival. Early research in this field has shown that the brain responds to experience no matter if those experiences are positive or negative. We underestimate how important a simple human touch can be, but research is proving us wrong. Research on newborns has shown that untouched newborns had a 30% higher chance of dying than newborns who were touched (Spitz, 2017). It is no surprise then that being lonely and in social isolation can make us sick, cause mental health issues and substance use even to premature death (Ingram et al., 2020, Novotney 2019). Just think of the recent Covid-19 pandemic that caused many to isolate due to stay-at-home orders and physical distancing orders for weeks or months at a time. While only the future will show its long-term effects on our health, we do know based on survey results that 26% of young adults either started or increased substance use, had elevated mental health conditions like anxiety and depressive disorder, and even had suicidal ideation (Czeisler et al. 2020). We are simply wired to connect with others and cannot find happiness and comfort in solitude. Our deep biological need for love has helped humanity survive for thousands of years. It played a crucial role in the survival of our ancestors and the reason you and I exist on this earth today.

4.2. Riding the Waves: Building Resilience Through Self-Love

Self-love and emotional resilience are crucial components of emotional well-being and living a healthy life. With a strong sense of self-worth and acceptance, people can navigate life's challenges with greater ease. By promoting self-love and resilience, we can help our teens stay away from the drug culture and resist peer pressure. Self-love is treating oneself with kindness, compassion, and acceptance. Self-love has nothing to do with external factors. It comes from within. It is the recognition of internal worth and treating oneself as a best friend despite mistakes and setbacks. Practicing self-love involves a range of activities such as eating healthy foods, exercising, meditation, positive self-talk, or setting healthy boundaries with others. When people ask me, what self-love really means, this is what I tell them.

"Self-love means that you love yourself so much, that you would not do anything that would hurt you."

A terrific way to teach them the importance of self-love is by modeling it with your own actions and behaviors. It includes your daily habits like your diet, work ethic, physical exercise, and how you solve conflicts. It also includes how you tackle your own responsibilities and obligations. Most importantly, teach your child to love themselves the way they are and who they are. Help them develop a positive body image. Make them understand that the bodily changes that they experience are normal and natural. Foster healthy habits that can help them feel more confident and more comfortable in their own skin. This includes teaching them to focus on their strengths rather than on their weaknesses. The biggest form of self-love is to foster a growth mindset. It is the belief that our abilities can be developed with dedication, effort, and hard work. Those who love themselves want the best for themselves and they put in the effort to overcome challenges and learn to become their best and truest selves. Let your child know that their human potential is limitless and the importance of chasing big goals. Be empowering! Do not be miserly with your compliments. Encourage and praise hard work, bravery, and effort when appropriate. Everyone likes a pat on the back and being acknowledged. You can even praise your child for a desired behavior you want him to demonstrate. Research has proven that this does indeed work, a phenomenon called '**alter casting**'. Praising or attributing someone for a favorable trait is likely to motivate the receiver to live up to your praise (Cialdini 2021; Cialdini et al., 1998). For example, you can praise saying things like 'I like how you finish what you start', 'you are always so kind and helpful'. Just watch your child demonstrate exactly the traits you want him or her to do even more. It will work like magic.

Make clear that they are allowed to make mistakes and grow from them. The best way to teach is to lead by example. Demonstrate that problems are an opportunity to learn and not a permanent defeat. You can openly discuss how to best solve a particular problem by brainstorming with your child. Helping them use self-talk is a great way to teach resilience despite adversity and the best way to do that is by modeling it. Remember, our "mini-me's" are watching even though we sometimes think they are not. Here are a few examples you can pass on:

- I did not like what happened, but I sure learned a lot.
- I will continue working toward my goals.
- There is always a way if I am committed.
- Do not panic! I got this.
- I am capable of handling this challenge.
- I have overcome challenges before, and I can do it again.
- I am in control of my thoughts, and I choose to focus on the positive.

Like Tony Robbins famously says, "Life is happening for me, not to me". This quote is changing my life for the better every single day. What used to bother me no longer has any power. And I will forever be grateful to him for this valuable lesson, and it is my honor to share it with you so you and your loved ones can experience its positive impact like I did.

Another useful method that I find highly effective is humor. I love making fun of myself when I make mistakes. I instantly shift my mood from negative to positive and it is a great lesson to pass on! It reduces the seriousness of the situation and stress, BUT it also reduces the feelings of despair and hopelessness. I call this a win-win. Teach your children very early on that failure is not a permanent defeat, but a natural part of life and that we learn and grow from. I invite you to watch Sara Blakely's inspiring video on YouTube. She is the founder of the company SPANX.

She openly shares the importance of taking risks and how her dad encouraged her and her brother to fail. Her father would even be disappointed if they did not fail at something that week because it simply meant they did not try (CNN Business 2018). Sara's dad sure understood that failure is a powerful teacher and that it can help build resilience and the mental muscle to bounce back from challenging setbacks. Why is resilience and self-love so important in the prevention of substance use in teens? When people are stressed and hopeless, they often reach for unhealthy coping mechanisms such as using drugs for emotional relief. Studies show that stress can have a negative effect at different stages during an addiction. For example, it can be the reason for drug use, the reason for relapse, and the reason for cravings (Koob and Schulkin 2019, Shoaib et al., 2018). Practicing self-love and resilience building tools are a powerful combination in the fight against stress and drug use not just for teens but for everyone.

4.3. Correcting Our Wrongs

The best course to teach them, and this is crucial, is not to abuse any substances yourself. Not only you, but also your spouse or significant other or, for that matter, anybody in the household. I sometimes get the question; how do you explain your own substance use behavior to your children? I challenge you to consider using yourself as an example if you have ever struggled in the past with a history of substance use. Some parents are hesitant to share out of shame and embarrassment. I do not blame them as you do not want to give them the impression that it is acceptable to use drugs since you did it too. Your own struggles, the impact of the wrong peer group, lack of guidance by parents, and how you overcame your struggle can all be useful tools to teach based on your own experiences. If you did anything stupid in your youth, share it! If it helps your child avoid the same pitfalls you fell into in the past, teach them how you got there. Most importantly, how you got out. Use your own judgment by making this decision about how your child may perceive this news. If you choose to honestly share your own experiences with using drugs, tell them that it was a mistake and the adverse effects it cost you. Say something like "It was stupid of me; I never want you to make that mistake too". But know that you will lose all credibility by exaggerating the effects of alcohol and telling them to never ever drink if you enjoy a glass of your favorite alcoholic beverage now and again. This is not "do as I say, not as I do". But if you are a responsible consumer yourself, you will teach your child exactly that. To be responsible. You can point out that adults are allowed to have a glass of their favorite alcoholic beverage occasionally and that they can do as well when they turn 21. Use moments like these also to raise awareness of dangerous facts, for example, that driving under the influence is an absolute taboo and they should never drive or get in a car with someone under the influence.

I also want to be clear and straightforward about one thing and I know there are people out there who need to hear this: If you are a parent that is abusing drugs and you are reading this book to help your child, get help first! (Visit FindTreatment.gov to find a center near you). Become the inspiration your child needs. Be a positive influence and a good role model. Lead by example and be the trigger for their own journey to recovery. Once you free yourself from your own addiction, you have demonstrated and become proof that it is possible. Why am I bringing up this subject? Children are great at modeling behavior. There are some family factors that increase the likelihood of a teen suffering from a drug addiction. This increases the risk of our own future drug use, making it a generational problem. Several research findings found common family characteristics of adolescents abusing substances and found the following risk factors. Among those are:

- Having parents who were using alcohol themselves.
- High conflict in the family
- Parents show a positive attitude about alcohol.
- Parents making access to alcohol easy.
- Parents and adolescence lacking quality relationships.

Just being aware of these risk factors can help you take proper action by improving parental behavior and seeking formal intervention to address the problem. Children are literally 'interns' they learn by watching. Furthermore, substance use by parents significantly increases the likelihood of child physical abuse, emotional abuse, and neglect (Kepple 2018). I have seen many devasted parents whose children were removed from parental home by Child Protective Services temporarily as well as permanently. Look, we all screw up from time to time. Do not get into self-blaming negative talk such as 'I should have done that' or 'I could have done this'; it is wasted time and energy. You cannot undo what happened in the past, but you can help your child's recovery and help shape their future. Be a part of the solution and let go of what you did wrong. Just the fact that you are reading this book is proof that you are a loving and caring parent looking for ways to help your teen the best way possible.

4.4. How Mentors Can Guide the Way

You are not the only source of influence and inspiration. Other family members, peers, schools, and your community are all powerful sources that can help prevent youth from engaging in drug use. They need to be exposed to strong targeted messages delivered consistently and repeatedly. Having mentors has huge benefits when it comes to building a strong support system and social network. They do not have to be the most accomplished family members or people in the community. They just need to be someone with a positive attitude or growth mindset who are good role models and whom your child can trust and be open. Someone that does not use drugs and can help shape their worldview in a positive way. Experts have studied the impact that adult mentors can have as a prevention strategy for substance use and here is what they found: "natural or informal mentoring showed significant positive effects... Building on youth's existing social resources and contacts with adult role models may be an important resource for preventing adolescent substance use" (Office of Juvenile Justice and Delinquency Program 2020).

This is exactly why I found success in influencing young minds with whom I work. I openly share my experiences and struggles as a teen, and we can relate with each other. I see myself in them, because I have walked in their shoes, and they see what can become of them with hard work and determination by listening to my story. Growing up, I had no mentors who could teach and show me the way. As someone who grew up with extreme low self-esteem and self-worth, I educated myself in self-improvement and growth just by listening and watching motivational videos on YouTube. Within a few years, I became an author of multiple books and became an expert in high performance skills and substance use. I tested every high-performance skill I teach to others on myself first. Now I can use my skills to mentor and teach others failproof and simple mind hacks and tricks they can apply immediately and see results. This helps them build confidence, elevates their mood, and helps them take a step toward their best self. They discover the strength within, feel pride, and realize the human potential that gives them hope and courage to reach higher. This is the most powerful way of prevention. By channeling their energy and focus on their goals and a better future, we create a 'natural high' that comes from pride and excitement. They will no longer feel the need to reach out for the fake 'artificial highs' of drug use.

I know that some parents work long hours and have limited time to spend and to meet their child's needs. Find mentors in your community, not to replace you or take over your parental duty, but to team up with you to create an added social support for your child's well-being. Even if you cannot find anybody in person, there are plenty of resources online that substitute as a mentor and role model. (At Mentoring.org you can search for a mentor near you or sign up to become a mentor). There are many inspirational and motivational videos, movies, books, seminars, masterminds, webinars, or courses that are available. That is exactly how my journey to self-improvement started. Just be resourceful and creative in your search.

Always welcome

under my wings.

Chapter Five

HOW TO RAISE DRUG-FREE CHILDREN IN A DRUG-FILLED WORLD

5.1. The Art of Listening and Connecting with Your Child

Parents are sometimes so busy working to support their families that many forget how important it is to carve out quality time with their children. You need to find a happy balance between work and family and intentionally put aside a specific time of the day to just be present and listen to your child. Work on building a strong foundation for a healthy relationship and not just when things start to go wrong. It will help strengthen the quality of your relationship and foster a deeper connection and bonding between you both. A crucial part of bonding is active listening. Listen and give them your undivided attention, and show interest in their lives, and ask questions. Because asking questions shows that you are interested and that you care about their experiences and well-being.

Ask open-ended questions or use topics from the news or movies to discuss topics like drugs, sex, the influence of friends, or other social issues. Listen actively and show interest in their world. If they ask questions that you do not know the answer to, research the subject together to find out. Make even small moments count, whether at the dinner table or chaperoning in the car, and ask questions like

- 'What lesson did you learn today?'
- 'What was the highlight?'
- 'What are your plans for the weekend?'
- 'What made you happy and what was upsetting?'

These types of questions will help your child to share their thoughts and feelings. Putting their emotions and thoughts into words will give them the opportunity to let negative emotions out instead of holding on in silence. Everyday moments like these may seem insignificant, but they are worth pure gold. It gives them permission to speak their mind and express their feelings. It also gives you a window of opportunity to share your wisdom and make your child feel 'felt', 'heard', and 'loved'. Listen without interrupting, be understanding and empathetic. Sometimes children can get a thrill out of breaking the rules just for fun. They want to make parents pay for being strict and controlling with the moto 'I am breaking your rules and you will never find out'. You cannot win by making them feel bad about themselves, making them feel not good enough, or not smart enough. What you do not want is to give them a reason to reach out to emotional band aids such as drugs to suppress unpleasant feelings.

A great way to connect with your child is also sharing things about your own day and experiences. These can be funny or unpleasant events that you can share, how you solved an issue or problem. Ask for your child's advice by saying 'what would you have done?', 'what do you think I could have done differently, to prevent ... from happening?". As much as you want to be a part of their lives, make them a part of yours and help them develop thinking and problem-solving skills at the same time. The quality of your relationship with your child is extremely important. If they do not have a healthy relationship with you (or someone who fulfills the role of a primary caregiver), they will find a substitute. Unfortunately, drugs become the substitute for many. The good news is: There are always ways to improve your relationship with your child, no matter how strong or strained it might be. Let me give you a few simple tips as inspiration:

- **Keep the Communication Channels with Them Open:** This means that your child needs to be comfortable sharing with you anything that bothers him/her. This helps build trust. With trust they are more likely to express their true thoughts, feelings, and experiences. With open and supportive communication, they are more likely to feel safe enough to share good news as well as unpleasant ones. And this will give you the opportunity to identify and address any issues early in the process.

- **Do Not Make Them Fear You:** Your child should respect you but not be afraid of you. They will not share with you their issues and problems if they fear your reaction and punishment. If they cannot talk to you, they will go someplace else. You do not want your child to go to others for advice who lack wisdom or who may not have their best interest in mind. I understand that some parents want to protect their children as much as possible by being strict and firm. However, if your child starts to fear you, then you both will lose. It is important to set rules and expectations for responsible and acceptable behavior and still have a loving and supportive relationship at the same time.

- **Love on Them:** Show and express your unconditional love. Children need and crave attention and if they do not get any, they know how to get it with misbehavior. For many, negative attention is better than no attention at all. Children want to be heard, understood, seen, felt, and loved! Listen actively without judgment and criticism. A hug can go a long way and sometimes it is really all they need!

- **Show Respect:** Treat your child with respect no matter their age. This includes respecting their thoughts and feelings. Any criticism needs to be constructive so he/she can learn to correct a certain behavior without attacking their character. Give constructive feedback when appropriate without judgment and blame. By making comments like 'how can you be so stupid', can have a permanent negative effect on your relationship.

- **Joint Activities:** A good way to connect and build a healthy and strong relationship with your child is to spend more one-on-one quality time and doing fun activities together. This can include anything that you two loves doing like eating out, going to a theme park, taking part in a group workout at a gym, or simply walking at a nearby park. If you have no joint hobbies or activities you like, I suggest you pick an activity that your child prefers. Make sure the fun activities are reserved to connect and to have fun only. Avoid talking about any problems or issues that could spoil the moment that is reserved only to make lasting memories. Tip: If you have more than one child, it is important that you carve out special 'fun' time for each one on a regular basis. They all have different needs and wants, the need for love and connection, and they long for your undivided attention.

- **Stay Engaged:** Be resourceful and find ways to stay engaged, spend quality time, and simply be a part of your child's world. Play games, watch a movie, go to concerts or the theater. This will not only strengthen your bond but will also create lasting memories. The Covid-19 pandemic changed the way people work in many ways. Many jobs can now be performed from home. Speak to your employer to see if you have the choice to work from home on some days. Just being home more often gives extra opportunities to spend time with your child.

- **Protect From Harm:** Protect your child from chronic stress, trauma, or any kind of violence. Chronic exposure to stress, or toxic stress, during childhood was associated with early initiation of drug use, substance use disorder, relapse, risky behavior, and early morbidity and mortality (Amaro et al., 2021, Campbell et al., 2016). But I would like to highlight the importance of NEVER abusing or neglecting your child, not physically nor mentally. Not by you, nor other family members, friends, acquaintances, or your spouse. This includes any kind of humiliation, put-downs, or other degrading behavior. If you are witnessing harm to your child and find yourself helpless to protect them or to prevent it, call Child Protective Services at once! While some stressors will be out of your control, your quality of connection and care can be a strong buffer to protect your child's well-being.

5.2. Educate Yourself on the Harm of Substance Use

Have you ever wondered how to prevent children from the exposure to drugs in today's drug filled society? We live in a world where drug use is prevalent. It is best to avoid the negative consequences from substance use and addiction before it has a chance to cause havoc or damage to individuals and families. The environment has a big influence on us and can make or break anybody. It is the environment that shapes our worldview, habits, and behaviors. You can imagine the environment as a sculptor that molds and shapes who we will become. The earlier you start teaching your children on the dangers of using drugs and its harmful effects, the higher the odds that they will avoid drugs and make healthy choices for themselves.

Like the famous quote of Benjamin Franklin says, "An ounce of prevention is worth a pound of cure". This quote is so true. It is better to prevent drug use from happening in the first place than trying to fix the damage that has already occurred. As we have discussed in Chapter 1.4., drug addiction is a chronic brain disease and recovery is a lifelong process. Simply put: Prevention can save a lot of pain and suffering, and any prevention attempt is worth the effort a million times. With the right strategies and approaches and ongoing effort, you can help your child learn skills that can help them make informed decisions. The goal is to prepare them for the world out there that is full of snakes. If you do not want your child to be bitten by the snakes disguised as humans, you need to protect them. Guard them with the necessary life skills to fight against the temptations of outside forces and pressure so they can make wise and responsible choices. You cannot be their guardian forever. My approach is instead of trying to overprotect and overcontrol them, teach them to think for themselves and make their own rational decisions.

An important step in educating your child on the dangers of substance use is to educate yourself first. I would like to congratulate you for taking the time to read this book. You are proving your commitment to help your teen overcome substance use or trying to learn ways to prevent it from happening in the first place. In either case, I hope you will find the inspiration to guide your teen to a healthier life. Remember, we cannot start early enough. Drugs in all their forms are so readily available. They are even available in school yards, so parents need to start educating themselves on the dangers of substance use way before they reach their teen years. Often parents start educating and learning about drugs long after the horse is out of the barn, as it were. Please, I implore you, do not wait! It is so much easier to do simple research that used to take us hours in the not-so-distant past. The Substance Abuse and Mental Health Services (SAMHSA) has created a very useful mobile app called "**Talk.**

They Hear You."® (2022). It is designed to help prepare parents, caregivers, educators, and communities for tough but important conversations around drugs. With interactive practice stimulation, videos, factsheets all the way to practicing what to say, it offers great tools to educate kids on drugs as well as underage drinking. Whenever opportunities present itself, have repeated and age-appropriate discussions on the dangers and harmful effects of drugs. Not just with words but show your child what it does to the body and people overall. The National Institute on Drug Abuse provides educational videos on different kinds of drugs as well as lesson plans and activity ideas for teachers and parents (http://nida.nih.gov/teens). Let them observe the reality of drug addiction. Sadly, there are many substance users on the streets that you can use as examples. Or simply google 'how people look when they take drugs', for example. You will be shocked! If this is not sickening and discouraging, I am not sure I know what is.

Again, do not differentiate between legal and illegal drugs. We have discussed this in Chapter 2.2, that even legal drugs can be harmful and even deadly. Stay informed about the latest drug trends. Google and Apple are not the only companies that keep on innovating. Criminal drug networks are innovating too. They are constantly working on creating more addictive, more colorful, better tasting, better smelling designer drugs in different forms and shapes that it can be hard to keep up. They are currently mass-producing deadly and fake prescription medications, like fentanyl and methamphetamine, and marketing them as legitimate prescription medications on social media and e-commerce platforms (Drug Enforcement Administration 2023). Regardless of what they come up with, by educating our teens on the dangers and risks associated with drug use and teaching them to live a healthy life, we can help them stay on a positive path and avoid falling prey to drug use. Knowledge is power but, in this case, your knowledge about drugs can save your child and your family from a lot of suffering. The best way to stay ahead of the game, regardless of what the drug market has to offer, is to lead by example. We can help our teens build their self-worth, resilience, and self-esteem that is unshakable by outside forces. Find ways to educate yourself on the dangers of drugs and continue promoting a drug-free behavior.

5.3. Help Build and Nurture Positive Relationships

As children enter their teen years, you will slowly lose grip, and they will no longer want to spend as much time with you. They would rather hang out with their friends and their plethora of tech gadgets. They want more independence and crave more autonomy. And that is perfectly fine. You need to loosen up the grip and give them the space to build their identity and independence. Friends are a valuable source as they grow their own identity and independence. They have a significant impact on their social and emotional development and course of life. Positive friends have positive effects on their physical and mental health and overall well-being. A compassionate ear in difficult times can provide them with the emotional support they need that can encourage them to stay resilient and push through.

People in their social circle have an impact on their behavior, thoughts, and feelings. Having positive friendships can reduce their risk of negative behavior and steer them toward making healthier choices. The latest research shows that the quality of their friendships with their friends can predict long-term outcomes than just their parents (Kelly 2021). Good teen friendships equal success later in life while not having good quality friendships shows the opposite effect. They showed poor work performance, were more likely to be depressed, and had poor quality relationships with others and with their romantic partners. It seems that the quality of their relationships in their teen years continues into adulthood. You play an important role in helping your child socialize with positive people and help them form healthy friendships. Here are some ways how you can help:

Provide Opportunities to Socialize: One effective way is to provide opportunities for your child to interact and socialize with their friends. You can organize and host social events such as sleepovers, invite friends on a day trip or to your house for some fun activities, have lunch or dinner, or arrange a fun movie night. Staying at a trusted friend's home also gives them the opportunity to socialize with friends and their families and can help them foster independence and self-esteem. Spending time with friends outside of school is a great way to strengthen and develop close friendships.

Part-time (or Full-time) Employment: It has many benefits and among those are building social and job skills, responsibility, and self-discipline. Earning their own money will help develop independence, confidence, and can help build financial responsibility early in life. While at the same time providing the opportunity to meet new people and expand their social network. It is also a great way to gain work experience that can then be used on their resumes and college applications.

Encourage Social Activities: Encourage your child to take part in social activities that align with their interests. Team sports, youth clubs, and volunteer organizations, where they have the opportunity to meet new people, are a great way for them to grow as a person. They develop social skills like communication, teamwork, empathy, or problem-solving skills. One of the fundamental needs of human nature is to belong and form social connections. Having a sense of belonging and acceptance in a group contributes to overall happiness and well-being. Not having a sense of belonging to a group can do the opposite: it can make people feel isolated, excluded, insecure, and have self-doubt. The feeling of being excluded is so painful that even brain imaging proves that it activates the same brain regions as a physical injury (Weir 2012). This can make them become vulnerable to develop various mental health issues such as depression and anxiety.

Promoting Independence: While it is important for teens to socialize with their peers, it is equally important to strike a balance between socializing and promoting their own independence. Allow them to explore their own unique interests and talents, try new hobbies or skills so they get a chance to discover their strengths. Create opportunities for them to engage in meaningful activities that bring them joy. They need to embrace their own individuality, take responsibility for their own behavior, and learn to make healthy choices. Mental toughness is an incredibly strong asset when it comes to resisting peer pressure and the urge to follow the crowd for validation.

Teach Values and Skills on Friendships: While we all want our children to have positive friendships and relationships, we cannot pick their friends for them. You can encourage and support them, but at the end of the day, they have the freedom to choose their own tribe. But what you can do is teach them to form healthy relationships by modeling them and to also discuss the values that belong in a healthy relationship. For example, discuss and show that a good friend is trustworthy, honest, encouraging, and supportive. And that they would not encourage you to engage in destructive and harmful behavior. Also discuss the negative attributes of bad friendships such as manipulation, jealousy, and dishonesty, which are overall a negative influence on their lives and future success.

5.4. The Cost of Negative Friendships

Who we are and who we will become is strongly influenced by our environment and the people in it. Especially during teen years, friends are incredibly important and can have a huge influence on their behavior, actions, values, and attitude. Friends provide guidance and support and help build their identity and self-esteem. We all are social creatures. We want to socialize and belong to a tribe. There is a popular saying 'you are the average of the 5 people you hang out with'. I totally concur with this statement. Hanging out with the wrong crowd is the easiest path to a troubled life. It is not rocket-science that if your child has 5 friends who consume drugs, he or she will be number 6 pretty soon. Using drugs with their friends feels like being on the same boat where they feel safe and accepted. The problem is that they do not see the problem when they are in the middle of it. They do not realize that this boat trip that feels so fun and harmless is actually a sinking ship pulling people down to misery. This is the perfect spot to use the phrase 'misery loves company' and so relevant as people who use drugs are drawn to others who are also using drugs. This is not only my opinion. This is a scientific fact. A research study has found that the substance use of a close friend predicted their own substance use. In addition, the researchers shared another interesting finding:

"Substance use by an individual close friend is an important influence on adolescent behavior regardless of whether the relationship between an adolescent and his/her friend is supportive full of conflict" (Branstetter et al., 2011).

As you can see, they do not even have to get along to engage in the same stupid behavior. Not only do the characteristics of a friend matter, but the quality of their friendship does as well. But that is not all. Researchers made another interesting discovery that is quite relevant to you as my target audience. The level of support from friends did not have an influence on their substance use behavior but the relationship with the mother did! A greater level of support from mom was linked to less frequent use of drugs and fewer negative outcomes. On the other hand, less support from mothers could predict increased use of hard drugs. A positive relationship with your child is an incredibly powerful tool to protect against using drugs. I am struck by the findings of this research, but not surprised. I decided to write this book just for moms because I know of their incredible powerful force and this book is a tribute to their unique power.

I have witnessed firsthand what a big impact friends can have on female offenders I had the pleasure to work with. I have learned that friends can be the reason to start using drugs and also be the reason for relapse. I cannot help but think of the term 'social comparison theory'. It is a theory in psychology that explains how individuals evaluate themselves by comparing themselves to others. By doing so, they can evaluate their own abilities, traits, appearance, and social status. When people compare themselves to others who are worse off, it is called 'downward social comparison'. When they compare themselves to others who are better it has the name 'upward social comparison'. As you can imagine, comparing to those who are worse off (inferior in status) makes people feel good about themselves and when comparing themselves to others who are better and more successful (superior in status) they can feel threatened, inadequate, or envious. It is a natural human tendency, and we all engage in it from time to time. This is how I explain this phenomenon to my clients in recovery:

"When you are recovering from using drugs, you climb the hierarchy ladder to a better you and leaving everyone behind who is still using. How do you think they feel about being left behind? Exactly. They will feel pretty bad about themselves because now they will have to look up to you when before you were on the same eye level. By getting you back into drug use, they pull you back down the ladder to make you be on the same eye level again. Mission accomplished!

Without exception, I can almost hear the alarm bell ring in their mind. They now see that it was not a good intention but a malicious act whether they realize it or not. My intention to explain this social comparison theory is not to make them hate their friends but to open their eyes and not fall into the trap the next time they are in similar risky situations. This is very similar to dieting. When someone knows that you are dieting and is still offering or even insisting that you have a piece of cake, I suggest you reevaluate your friendship with that person. This is not a good intention in my view. The proper approach should have been like this "No you cannot have a piece of cake (or drugs). Remember your goal and I want to help you reach it". See the difference? Do not miss the chance to have an open dialogue about peer pressure. Teach them drug refusal skills so they build the confidence and courage to say NO to everything that feels wrong, no matter what! It is also useful to practice and role-play how to say it like 'No, thanks. I will pass!', or to just simply walk away and leave the scene. This builds confidence and helps them prepare for real-life situations.

What we learn from our pain,

are lessons learned for

future gain.

Chapter Six

BREAKING THE CYCLE OF ADDICTION

6.1. Recognize Drug Use and Take Action Fast

My guess is if you have come this far in this book, you already know that there is a problem with drug use. Maybe you have been suspecting that something is going on for a while now. Maybe you simply did not want to believe it and were in a state of denial. It is common for parents to feel shame and guilt and even blame themselves for their child's addiction. But remember, you are just one piece of the puzzle. You can do all the right things and still have a child who is engaging in substance use. Act fast and stop the self-blame. Do not wait for the warning signs to be so obvious that your neighbor or friend tells you that there is something wrong. Not accepting reality is one of the main reasons why families fail to respond promptly. We do not want our world to fall apart, and we do not feel equipped to cope and deal with this situation. It is easier to rationalize the problem by hoping that they will "grow out of" substance use as they mature and transition into adulthood. Maybe you too are wondering how your child who was always a good kid, nice, and respectful, could possibly engage in drug use. But it happens. It is easier to intervene at earlier stages of addiction before they are hooked. Data shows that many adults struggling with drug addiction have begun using drug addiction in their teen years

(Chakravarthy et al., 2013). Early detection and intervention also mean saving precious time and minimizing long-term effects before the toxic chemicals can cause much damage to the person's life and body. Drug addiction carries a high risk for poor school performance, delinquency, teen pregnancy, and depression (Belcher and Schinitzky 1998). It is easier to remove cancer when it is still small than waiting for it to metastasize and kill you for sure. For you to intervene and help your child, you first need to find out and know which drug is being used. They are so smart and good at masking their drug use to avoid getting caught, that it can be challenging to find out the signs of drug use. They do not necessarily use their parental home for drug use, often instead using a friend's home, parties, at night when everyone is sleeping, when parents are away, or in public. Just asking them if they are using drugs will often not help you find out the truth. Many lie out of fear. That is why I would like to raise awareness of some red flags that can help indicate drug use.

Paraphernalia: Substance uses leaves clues and these clues come in the form of utensils called 'drug paraphernalia'. Those can be anything that is used to prepare or consume drugs. Many of the items are everyday items but in totally wrong locations. For instance, what is aluminum foil doing in your child's room or car? Or a Q-tip in his or her pocket? Why would anyone need numerous lighters in multiple locations? Forks, pipes, bongs, syringes, rolling paper, or a gas burner are all tools used to prepare and consume drugs. Sometimes strings or similar items are carried as tourniquets. They are used to expose engorged veins to inject the drug such as heroin. Other signs can be a powdery residue on identification cards or credit cards, rolled up money or half of a straw to inhale the drug through the nose. Also watch out for new habits such as excessive use of breath mints or chewing gum to cover up the odor of certain drugs or alcohol.

Clothing: Examine your child's clothing. This is especially easy if your child is living with you, and you are the one doing his or her laundry. Look out for any burn holes or other holes on clothing, carpet, or bedding. Holes for example can be the sign of cigarette use or other drugs that are consumed with a pipe like marijuana, crack cocaine, or methamphetamine. Some drugs (i.e., opioids, cocaine) cause compulsive itching that people scratch themselves so intensely, that it can leave holes, tears, or blood stains on their clothes. Blood stains on clothing can also indicate the use of drugs by injection. If you notice the same type of blood stain in the same location (i.e., sleeves, cuffs) repeatedly, this may be a sign that drugs are being injected into the arm on a regular basis. Also keep an eye out for any hidden pockets sewn into the lining of clothing that are sometimes used to conceal drugs or store drug utensils.

Physical Warning Signs

When drugs become a priority, everything else is secondary. They do not keep up with their appearance. They will neglect grooming and hygiene and often look sick, have dark circles under the eyes, suffer from acne, or carry an odd smell. The outside can mirror the inside. How we look mirrors what is occurring on the inside. I have never seen someone with a serious drug addiction look their best. It is always the opposite. They look older, sick, and simply miserable. You may also notice a loss of appetite, significant weight loss, nosebleed, tooth decay (common problem caused by using methamphetamine), burns on fingers and lips. People who use methamphetamine often feel the sensation as if drugs are crawling underneath their skin, a condition called 'crank sores'. Excessive picking and scratching can cause open sores, skin lesions, or infections.

Behavioral Warning Signs

Drug addiction does more damage than just on the physical appearance. It changes the character and the mental state, always in a negative way. They can become unrecognizable. It is extremely painful to watch a loved one lose positive qualities such as honesty, trustworthiness, positivity, and sincerity. Replaced by skillful lies and manipulation, theft, robbery, burglary, anxiety, aggression, and delinquency. You may also notice that items start missing in the house or that your loved one is selling personal belongings that are of value. This could mean that valuables are sold in pawnshops to buy drugs. Addiction is not only dangerous, but also expensive. They become secretive and it is easy to confuse this with their high need for privacy at this age. By trying to cover up their drug use, they tell one lie after the other that just does not make any sense. The explanations just do not add up if you dig a little deeper with a few more questions. Watch out for the following abnormal behavioral signs. These can be anything that is not typical, unusual, or odd such as:

- Fidgety or hyperactive
- Depressed or anxious
- Paranoia, delusions, panic attacks, or mental confusion
- Frequent night activity
- Laughing flashes (that is odd or unusual)
- Extreme drowsiness
- Teeth grinding
- Neglecting responsibilities
- Withdraws from family and 'non-using' friends
- Declining school performance, poor grades
- Poor concentration/memory
- Constantly asking/borrowing/needing money (Are you checking how they spend it?)
- Missing school/workdays
- Hanging around with the wrong crowd, people known for drug use or illegal activity
- Wearing long sleeves on a hot day (just does not make sense). May try to cover up intravenous drug use or scars on arms from scratching (crank sores)
- Extreme mood-swings
- Avoiding eye contact
- Impaired/enhanced movement, difficulty walking
- Slurred/frenzied speech
- Nausea and vomiting, especially after a night out
- Missing cash or valuables
- Depletion of checking/savings accounts

Tip: Just to be on the safe side, learn CPR as soon as possible. You want to be prepared to help a loved one (or anybody in need) if you are ever faced with a tragic emergency. Visit Redcross.com to find a CPR and First Aid course you can attend in person or online.

If you can relate to some of the warning signs above, do not panic. Maybe the warnings sign you picked up on have nothing to do with drug use. But do not ignore them either. But there must be a reason for the recent changes. Is it a breakup, bullying, family issues? If you think something is off, trust your intuition because it usually is correct. Drug addiction ruins so many families not just emotionally, but also financially. To limit financial damage, I encourage you to freeze your child's savings account or cancel mutual bank or credit cards and keep your valuables like jewelry in a locked or safe place, ideally at a bank. You need your recourses to finance rehabilitation, counseling, or treatment and not put it in the pockets of drug dealers.

6.2. Confrontation: Help Your Child to Say YES to Recovery

*L*et us suppose that you have discovered that your child is abusing drugs. Now what do you do? Panic, anger, fear, disappointment, and confusion are normal emotions that, without question, all moms experience. It is a mother's instinct to desperately want to help and protect her young. I would like to warn you that screaming, yelling, insulting, threatening, physical or verbal abuse is not going to help. Share your suspicion and worries with your spouse or partner or someone you feel close to that can provide emotional support. The best approach is to have an open and honest conversation with your child. I know you have a million questions that you want to ask, but you cannot ask them all at once. Trust me, I know this is easier said than done. But also trust me, you will have more success using the methods discussed in this chapter than yelling, screaming, or giving a spanking.

Confrontation should not be a cross-examination a la Columbo style, but rather an open dialog to start the discussion on this important issue. Your child may get scared, mad, or angry that you found out about it. But the warmer and more comforting the first conversation is, the second one is likely to get better as well. Before you start the confrontation, here are a few tips that can help you prepare. It is not just about what to say, but also about how you say it:

- **Choose the Right Time:** It will not have the desired effect if you say the right thing at the wrong time. Find a time when the two of you can have an uninterrupted conversation without being distracted.

- **Use 'I' Statements:** By using 'I' statements, you can express your concern without judging, accusing, or blaming. Avoid using 'you' in your statements because it is accusatory in language. It can make your child become defensive, feel criticized, and attacked. This could lead to a heated argument which is exactly what you want to avoid. For example, do not say 'How can you do this?". Instead, say things like 'I am concerned about you'. Voice your worries without attacking and scaring your child. Your child needs assurance that you are on his or her side and not the enemy in which to run.

- **Ask Open-Ended Questions:** Notice these ice breakers are all open questions. Express how you feel and give them the opportunity to do the same. You want to avoid closed-ended questions that can be answered with a simple yes or no. You want your child to give you information to find out what is going on in your child's life.
- **Just Listen:** Even if you do not like what you are hearing, just listen and try to understand your child's feelings and perspective. Make sure not to interrupt, make a disgusted face, or roll your eyes.

Just to give you an idea, here are some samples of ice breakers to bring up the subject of your child's drug use in a gentle and calm way without shaming and/or blaming:

- Can we talk for a minute? **I am concerned** about you, and I would like to talk to you about what you have been going through lately. I have a feeling that something is not right. Please share with me how you are feeling.
- **I am worried** about you. I noticed some drastic changes in (mood/grades/appetite/weight/peer group…)
- **I know** you are going through some tough times lately. What can I do to help you feel better?
- **How can I help** solve the problem you are dealing with?
- **I noticed** that you are taking some substances that are extremely harmful and dangerous to your health. This is absolutely unacceptable. I will not allow you to hurt yourself.

- **I know it is hard** to talk about this, but I need to know what kind of drugs you used.
- You know that **I always appreciate** your honesty. Please tell me what exactly you are taking, when you started, and how often you use it. And I promise, I will not punish you for your honesty. I may have lost my temper in the past, but I apologize for it. I am not here to make you feel miserable. I am really here to help.
- **I want to help you**. Here are some options (i.e., rehab, counseling) which one do you prefer? Do you have a better idea or suggestion? We can work together to find an agreement!
- You know that **I love you**. I will help and support you get through this anyway I can. Do not be afraid. We will figure out a solution together and find the help that you need. If you do not feel comfortable talking to me about certain issues, I can help find a professional to whom you can talk.

Regulate – Relate - Reason

When it comes to discussing your child's drug use, the quality of your conversation will depend on several factors like the current circumstances, the quality of your relationship, and the emotional state of the two of you. When your child is ready to talk, show empathy and actively listen (do not think about what you are going to say), stay present, and definitely do not interrupt. Wait for a natural pause before responding. Your response to your child's statements is extremely important. If you sound too controlling, it will push them away and they will become defensive and shut down. With the proper communication strategy, you can create a supportive and non-judgmental environment for them to open up, instead of pushing them away. One effective strategy I find very effective is to use the reflective-listening method in combination with Dr. Bruce Perry's method of communication he developed. Dr. Perry is a child psychiatrist, neuroscientist, and expert in childhood trauma. His method involves 3 Steps: Regulate, Relate, and Reason (also called the three R's) (Perry and Winfrey 2021). The 3 R's is a popular framework that is used in conflict resolution, in reaching mutual understanding, or agreement. The three components of this method are:

1. **Regulate** The first step is to regulate your child 's emotions and calm them down. He or she may be upset, scared, or frightened. Restate what he/she had said in your own words in a non-judgmental, soothing, and non-critical way. This shows that you actively listened and are trying to understand their perspective. This is also called **reflective listening**. By helping them to calm down, you help turn off your child's fight-flight or freeze response. This is important because when they are scared, angry, or stressed, the thinking part of the brain, the cortex, will shut down. You will not be able to get through to them. Our brain is organized in such a way that we feel before we think. If you want your child to think clearly, you need to first make sure they feel calm, safe, and connected to you. Emotions are contagious. If you stay calm,

it is likely your child will mirror it. A great way to regulate may be to give your child a hug or hold their hand.

2. **Relate:** In this step, you relate to your child by acknowledging and validating their feelings, challenges, perspective, and experiences. When you actively listen and express empathy without judgment and criticism, your child will feel heard, understood, and loved. This will help create a safe and supportive environment for healthy communication.

3. **Reason:** Now that they are calm, you can use reasoning by explaining your own point of view and the reason behind it. According to Perry, when they are calm, their cortex, the thinking and reasoning part of the brain is at work. Now they can use their cognitive skills to understand your perspective and be able to discuss the issue of drug use. You can now explore the reasons behind your child's drug use (i.e., peer pressure, stress, thrill-seeking) and discuss the harm and risks associated. You can further work on constructing a potential solution and plan of action such as stopping drug use, treatment, changing the environment, coping strategies, etc. The goal is to help them recognize the negative consequences and risks to their health and their life, so they seek and want help for their own well-being.

Here are a few examples:

Your child: "It was calming and fun at first. Everyone was doing it."

You: "I know drugs can have those calming effects at that moment. I can imagine you were scared when things got out of hand. Just because everyone was doing it does not mean it is harmless. I need you to stay away from drugs, no matter what your friends choose to do."

Your child: "I do not see what is wrong with using it occasionally. I can stop any time I choose."

You: "Maybe you do not see anything wrong with it, but drugs are extremely dangerous. Have you thought of its potential dangers? Have you tried to quit before? (If the answer to this question is yes, ask further!) What happened that made you start using it again? I would like us to do some research. You will see for yourself how even occasional use can cause you harm."

Your child: "I am not doing anything wrong. Just leave me alone"

You: "Please calm down. I know you are a good child and are very smart. I understand that you want to make your own decisions. But I am your mom and I love you. You must trust me. It is my responsibility to voice my worry and concern about your drug use. Drugs affect the brain and can cause long-lasting damage. They are very addictive. I do not want you to destroy your life. Think of all the plans you have for your future."

Your child: "I am scared. I do not need therapy. I want to stay home."

You: "I know you are scared. I totally understand your worry. But there is a way out. There are great treatments, and they are very good at helping people recover from drugs. We will find the right help for you. Everything will be fine."

Your child: "I was so stressed out because of _________ (school, breakup, parents, etc.) "

You: "I know you were stressed about___________. It was a rough time for you. I can imagine how you felt. Being stressed is not an excuse to take drugs and it is definitely not the solution to any problem. We can find a way for you to deal with stress better next time".

Your child: "It is all ______________ fault" (friend, divorce, neighbor, etc.)

You: "I am sorry you feel that way. I understand your frustration with___________. But I do expect you to take responsibility. Drugs can ruin your life and I want the best for you. Promise me you will never do it again!".

If you notice that your child is getting fearful, upset, angry, hysterical, and defensive, back off. Those emotions are crippling. Fear and anxiety shut down the cortex, the thinking part of the brain (Perry and Winfrey 2021). You simply will not go through a frightened child or somebody who is currently under the influence of substances and force them to make the right decision right there and then. Before we are able to think, we act and feel first. You can pick up the conversation the next day, when things settle down. You can say something like, "I understand it is a difficult topic and it seems like we are not on the same page right now. I am hopeful we can find a solution that works well for both of us. When is a good time to continue this conversation?". Try to negotiate and find a middle ground and a way to proceed with treatment and recovery, should it be necessary. Your child may not like the idea of getting professional help and may even deny that there is a problem at all. If your child expresses a desire to stop drug use and sounds determined in doing so, consider giving them time to reflect and the opportunity to change their behavior. To take action requires motivation and self-reflection and that is an internal process. Give your child the space to come to terms with reality. Pushing them too far too soon and forcing them to take immediate action can backfire, as it can lead to resistance and resentment toward change. If having healthy communication between the two of you is a challenge, consider writing a letter or email to express your worry and concern. It has the benefit that you can carefully choose your words and help you avoid saying things out of anger.

Tip: It is important to do damage control to find out what harm has happened, especially if drug abuse has been going on for a long period of time. Take your child to your primary care doctor for a thorough check-up. Just to be on the safer side, make sure testing for Hepatitis B and C, and sexually transmitted diseases like HIV is done. Because drugs affect judgment and decision-making, it is likely that they engage in high-risk behaviors like unprotected sex, sharing needles, or other drug paraphernalia.

If you are certain about the fact that your child is using drugs, you may be wondering how best to move forward. Maybe you are even wondering how serious the problem is and if it requires professional intervention. If you saw behavioral changes and have noticed a negative impact on your teen's life, there is probably an urgent need to address this issue. Even minor or occasional use of drugs can be a reason for concern. Even those small amounts can be risky and lead to escalation. I would highly suggest you consult with a healthcare professional to accurately assess your teen's situation. Parents feel stuck between trying to get help for their child on the one hand and trying to help the teen recognize the problem. It is another big challenge. Your perception of the problem will likely differ from your child's perception of the problem. You may see a problem– they may not. They either do not see the problem, are in denial, or are wishful thinking. Rarely do they think they need any kind of intervention or treatment or are too embarrassed or ashamed to admit that they do. This can be frustrating when efforts by parents are met with denial or resistance. They may try to cover it up or downplay their drug use by saying things like

- 'Chill out, it was just one time'
- 'Everybody is doing it'
- 'Do not worry, I will not get addicted'
- 'I can stop whenever I want, I do not any need help'
- 'Do I look like an addict to you?'
- 'Just leave me alone. I am just fine'

They can be very convincing and good at downplaying their drug use behavior. As much as you want to believe them and keep your world intact, be realistic and do not ignore the red flags and warning signs. Teens are known for their risk-taking behavior and for feeling invincible and untouchable as if nothing bad can happen to them. Do not fall for their illusion of control when they are actually losing it. There is significant risk in tolerating and looking the other way and excusing the substance use behavior to the experimentation period of teenagers. Even occasional use or in small doses does not guarantee that your child will not get harmed by the toxic chemicals that invade the brain and body. It can have risky consequences that can harm their health and well-being, like driving under the influence, unprotected sex, violence, or aggression that can have legal consequences. No mother wants to wait and watch their child freefall to misery beyond repair. It does not make sense to wait for your child to 'feel like it' or 'feel ready'. It is a waste of valuable time. Addiction does not simply fade away on its own. In Chapter 1.2., we used the analogy of a broken car brake. The brake will not fix itself without going to the mechanic. The same is also true for drug addiction. Tolerating drug use is like allowing your child to go swimming with the sharks and hoping they will not get eaten by them. Is it really worth taking the risk?

6.3. Evidence-Based Approaches to Motivate Behavior Change

The Path to Least Resistance

Have you ever wondered why teens hate to be told what to do? How can you motivate them to seek recovery? Once they perceive that you are trying to control their behavior and actions, it is as if they intentionally prefer to do the opposite. There is a way you can PERSUADE your child without making them feel controlled. The primary goal is to trigger a change in your child, so they WANT recovery and WANT to quit drug use. Teens hate to feel controlled. Either they resist and do it anyway or they quit out of fear or simply to get you off their back. But they continue the behavior clandestinely. While helping them make the right choice, you can gently influence them without making them feel controlled. Here is an example of how you can accomplish it:

Give your child a choice that is outrageously unattractive that he or she is likely to reject. You then present an alternative that is more attractive and a benefit in comparison to the first one. If your child is terrified of going to inpatient rehab, you can present inpatient (likely to reject) first and give him or her a second option which is to enter an outpatient program or a peer support group (likely to accept). This technique is based on the **'rejection-then-retreat technique'** combined with the **'perceptual contrast principle'**. Here is an example:

You: "I would like you to go to XYZ rehab center for 6 months in a different state"

Your child: Rejects the idea outright.

You: "All right, "If you promise to stay away from drugs and those sketchy friends, you can go to the outpatient program/peer support group in town."

Your child: He/she will agree as it will sound like a 'retreat' as compared to the first option. This second option is the one you wanted him or her to agree to in the first place.

For this method to work, you need to have a sense of what your child absolutely does not want. If your child prefers an inpatient treatment program or wants to move away, those will not be an unattractive choice at all. In contrast to the first one, the second offer will be perceived as a pretty good alternative (called the perceptual contrast principle). Just make sure that you are fine with either choice because in each case, nobody loses. Just choosing one of the options is still a win-win for you both. Tailor the options to your child's preferences and severity and inflicted harm of drug use. The goal is to move them to commit and take the road to recovery with the least amount of resistance.

The Power of Imagination

The power of imagination gives us the ability to envision our future by creating mental images, concepts, and ideas that are not present in the physical world. It is a rehearsal of a future event that could happen or prevent a desirable event from happening. It is so powerful because it gives us the ability to see what is possible even though it does not exist yet. It allows us to envision our goals and the life ahead. Use the power of imagination to make your child get excited about recovery. Make them imagine 'what could be'. You can guide your child to go on a journey and make him or her imagine a brighter future after recovery or a not-so-brighter future if continuing the use of drugs. You can say things such as:

- Just imagine never needing drugs again
- Imagine six months from now how your life will have changed when you begin treatment now?
- You can finally do all the things that you always wanted to do
- You can finally go back/finish/start school/work
- We will go on this trip and have an amazing time after you come back
- Imagine how life will be after step 1-2-3 are completed? Imagine these steps as a roadmap that leads to success.
- In one year from now, the issues of today will no longer matter. Just imagine what that will feel like.
- Imagine how continuing drug use will affect your future. Imagine the quality of your relationships, your education, and the impact on your goals. Just think of the quality of people that will surround you. Remember, any arrest and conviction can make it hard for you to find a job, join the military, or prevent you from pursuing your dream career.

- Imagine yourself ten years from now. Looking back, what would you tell your younger self? Where do you think you will be? What will you be doing? You can create that future self with your actions now.

What is great about our ability to imagine is that our brain does not know the difference between imagination and reality (Hétu et al., 2013). In both cases, it activates the same regions of the brain. Imagination can help prepare your child for the future. Imagination is like a movie that plays in your head. When you guide your child to picture a better life, it will make them vividly experience the future and make them look forward to recovery instead of dreading it. Conversely, imagining how life will turn out if drug use continues can be scary and terrifying. It is a useful technique to question their current behavior with drug use and what the road ahead will look like. Imagination can help them stay away from trouble. Just imagining the consequences of their actions and behavior can be a big help for them not to engage in those behaviors. It can also help them solve problems and make better decisions just by exploring in their own imagination the different scenarios and possibilities. This can trigger a new way of thinking and motivate them to change and wholeheartedly commit to recovery.

There are evidence-based approaches to motivate a teen to seek and stay engaged in their treatment. Some of them are:

Motivational Interviewing (MI)

Motivational interviewing is an evidence-based counseling practice to help individuals develop their own motivation (intrinsic motivation) and commitment to recovery. With the help of the therapist, they explore their ambivalence about behavioral changes. Rather than being told what to do, they are guided to explore their own feelings and thoughts to discover their own reasons for changing. They can also explore any conflicting feelings toward change. As an example, your child may want to continue using drugs but also have a strong desire to quit. The therapist can help address the ambivalence and skillfully guide them towards change. This can be an effective method with the help of a compassionate and empathetic therapist. Some teens (maybe all of them) do not like to be told what to do. They are likely to show resistance and rebel against traditional authority figures. By helping them identify the impact of their drug use on their own, they can find the motivation within themselves to change the behavior that is harming them. With open-ended questions and reflective listening, the individual identifies the problem as well as the solution for themselves.

Contingency Management (CM): This type of behavioral therapy uses rewards to promote positive behavior to make people stay committed to their treatment. Incentives are used as a tool to help them stay motivated by rewarding positive behavior. It can be in the form of prizes, vouchers, or other forms of incentives to make them follow through with treatment goals.

The goals, or desired outcomes, can be such things as attending treatment sessions as planned, passing drug tests, or staying drug-free. You know your child best. Collaborate with your child's treatment provider and identify meaningful rewards that can help your teen stay on track. This can be anything from gift cards, concert tickets, a small trip or vacation to a desired destination, or simply a fun shopping trip to the mall.

The ARISE ®Intervention Method

One promising intervention method is the ARISE® (a relational intervention sequence for engagement). Based on research data, it worked 83% of the time to motivate the addicted individual to start treatment (Landau & Garrett 2008). What is special about this method is that it uses motivational techniques and actively involves a strong network of family members and friends. Research data shows that it works better than confrontational intervention (based on criticism, guilt, shame, attack) and fosters long-term recovery (Garrett & Landau, 2010; Landau & Garrett, 2008). With the ARISE ® technique, individuals suffering from addiction first get 'invited' in a loving and welcoming way to start treatment. It seems to work so well because it gives people a sense of power and some control over the situation. By involving them in the process in a kind and gentle way, they do not feel any need to be defiant or rebellious. I know your parental instincts will want to grab them by the ear and drag them into treatment. Please do not do this. That falls under the confrontational method, and it will not work. Take a look at the ARISE ® approach that follows these three gradually escalating steps to motivate their loved one to enter treatment:

- **Level 1 'First Call':** Level 1 begins with a loved one (called 'concerned other') reaching out to an ARISE ® clinician mostly by an initial phone call. Strategies are discussed to motivate or 'invite' the substance user to attend the first meeting. You move to the next level if Level 1 does not work. Regardless of if the substance user attends the meeting or not, the meeting still takes place where further strategies to motivate the substance user are discussed.
- **Level 2:** During this stage, between 2-5 meetings are held before moving to the next level. Support groups in this approach work like a 'Board of Directors' and they collectively conduct intervention meetings. If after several meetings the individual did not enter treatment and continues using drugs, they move to Level 3.
- **Level 3 (Formal ARISE ®Intervention):** At this level, the 'Board of Directors' makes some tough decisions in terms of consequences if drug use has not ceased, or the person has not entered treatment yet.
- **Continuing Care:** After the onset of treatment, ongoing support and care are provided for 12 months to the individual and family to foster healing and recovery.
- (Visit Arise-Network.com to find a certified Arise® Interventionist)

CRAFT (Community Reinforcement and Family Training): This is a behavioral therapy approach designed to teach family members skills and strategies to encourage their loved ones to enter treatment and to stay engaged. Family members learn in a series of therapy sessions how best to support the individual in their treatment and in their journey to a lasting recovery.

Other Approaches: Other approaches such as family therapy, peer support groups (i.e., AA or NA), or cognitive behavior therapy (CBT) can also be an effective strategy to motivate treatment and to seek treatment. Resolving issues with family and improving communication and relationships is important. Identifying negative thoughts and behavior and learning new ways to cope and manage cravings and triggers, and being in a supportive peer support group can all be effective approaches to motivate your teen to seek treatment (please refer to 7.1. to learn about them). I've created a video specifically to inspire teens to overcome drug use, turn their lives around, and seek treatment – a vital message that could transform your child's life. Visit brightwingsandcoco.com to access this valuable resource.

6.4. The Double-Edged Sword of Using Force

Let us just assume your child is stubborn and chooses to resist any kind of treatment. How can you help someone who does not want to be helped? It can be frustrating to see them engage in the behavior despite knowing that it is hurting them. What should you do? Watch your loved one slip away in front of your eyes? Will you sit back and wait for your child to come to his or her senses? Would you even go as far as throwing your child out of your home to teach them a lesson or maybe to protect the well-being of your family? I certainly cannot tell you what to do as each case and person is unique, like a fingerprint. I can only encourage you to exhaust all options before taking drastic measures. In such extreme cases, keep in mind that kicking a child out of the house is a big decision and can be a paradoxical situation. There is a high chance that it can cause your child to slip deeper into the drug milieu, making them vulnerable to sexual and physical abuse and even prostitution. Keeping him or her home on the other side, you may put other family members' safety in jeopardy. Especially if drug addiction has made them become violent and uncontrollable. Pushing them away is not the solution. It only alienates them more, making them feel lonely, while giving them a strong reason to relieve the pain of alienation with drugs. You see, alienation is not making the problem miraculously go away, but it is actually making it worse.

Tip: If your child is violent toward you or another family member, call for immediate help (neighbor, friend, family member, or call 911) and get to safety.

I have seen time and again the kind of harm and abuse people on the streets are exposed. Whatever your decision may be, always weigh the pros and the cons. Also be reminded that kicking out an underage child is considered in most states to be child abandonment, and thus a crime. I would not recommend this avenue. Instead of kicking your child out, consider the possibility to use force with the help of law enforcement. If your child has reached dangerous levels of drug use and cannot be persuaded to enter rehab, they urgently need intervention. If all efforts have been exhausted, sending your child to involuntary treatment may be your last resort (always check your state's requirements and laws). This is so much better than kicking them out onto the streets and putting them in harm's way. But if force is truly the last resort, then so be it. It needs to be done. I want to warn you beforehand: They will not like this but who cares? I would rather visit my child at a rehab facility than at a cemetery. Plus, I would have the peace of mind of knowing that are getting the help they need and are in good hands. Again, check your state and local laws and make the best and smartest decision for your family. The National Institute on Drug Abuse states that for a treatment to be effective, it does not have to be voluntary (2018). I agree as I have seen this transformation firsthand. I have met inmates who were glad that they got locked up. It forced them to become drug free. For many it was a turning point in their life. They can finally pause, be still, and reflect on their life with a clear mind. They can see the self-destructive behavior that damaged them and their loved ones including parents, siblings, their children, relatives, and close friends. Hitting rock bottom is for many a well needed and eye-opening wakeup call. It is like coming back to reality from a nightmarish fantasy world. If this is something you would like to enforce, sometimes it helps to give them a warning ahead of time of your plan to use force, like calling the police. Just seeing that you mean it can motivate them to enter treatment voluntarily in order to save the humiliation of being apprehended and handcuffed.

Having said this, one major point to be aware of is not to confuse helping with enabling. You can help and support your child into recovery but do not become an enabler in the process. Bailing your child out 10 times is probably not a lesson your child can learn from. Neither is writing excuses for missed school days or covering up for other actions that would have been a good learning opportunity for your child. Without facing any consequences, there is no reason for them to stop their behavior. They will just continue to rely on you to clean up the mess. However, with consistent effort, the right support, and motivation, you can help your teen take important steps to a substance-free life. But remember, a shift happens slowly and gradually by taking one step and one day at a time. That is how momentum is built. Any progress is good news so do not miss any opportunity to encourage and praise your child for trying and improving their habits and behavior.

'I love you' and 'I'm sorry' are

both love languages.
Use them often.

Chapter Seven

TREATMENT OPTIONS AND RECOVERY FOR TEENS

Exactly what kind of recovery program is best for your child depends on the several factors: the severity of addiction, how long was the drug use occurring, what physical and psychological damage it has caused, etc. There are two paths to recovery, one being natural and the other formal recovery. While some individuals use the natural recovery route (also called 'cold turkey'), others need some form of formal assistance for recovery. When symptoms are mild, a strong will and commitment can help them to overcome an addiction on their own. Many do find the fuel for motivation after witnessing the negative consequences to their quality of life such as relationships, work, school, family, being arrested, or diminished health. Encourage your teen to detox in a supervised facility, especially for alcohol addiction. You cannot force somebody into a natural recovery if symptoms are so severe as it can be a painful process and difficult to watch. People with a serious drug addiction need a formal recovery program in the form of treatment by professionals. People who enter treatment want to get better. It requires courage and determination. Be ready for the emotional roller-coaster. Recovery is not a smooth highway and full speed ahead. It has lots of winding turns and potholes (setbacks) are common. Sometimes they take one step forward and three steps back but each time they fall back, they learn from their mistakes, build resilience, and begin to fall back less. Everyone's recovery journey is unique and not all of them advance at the same pace and in the same way.

What kind of treatment option is best for your loved one depends on several factors such as what kind of drug was used, how long it was consumed, mental and physical health, their own personal factors, and the severity of the addiction. You need to find the kind of help that makes sense depending on your child's unique needs and circumstances. Some with a strong will may manage to recover naturally without a formal support system. Yet others need a more structured intervention in the form of inpatient, outpatient, residential or other forms of treatment settings as recovery options. This is typically the case when they cannot quit on their own despite experiencing negative consequences such as to their health, relationships, work/school, or financial and legal problems. Make sure to consult with an addiction specialist to find out what treatment option is best for your child. Let us now review some common different treatment options.

7.1. Common Treatment Options to Overcome Addiction

Inpatient or Residential Treatment: Inpatient treatment is typically for teens with severe substance-use problems who need 24/7 structured and supervised support. Psychiatric and medical problems along with addiction are common. Individuals usually go through the detoxification (detox) process where the body is cleared of the toxins of drugs. Inpatient programs typically use a variety of treatment approaches. For example, medical and psychiatric care, group, and individual therapy, and counseling all the way to yoga, meditation, or nutritional counseling. This is critical. It takes more than detox to overcome addiction as psychological dependence will likely still persist. The unhealthy habits that lead the person to engage in drug use in the first place still linger around in the mind that still wants it. They need to learn healthy ways to experience pleasure and reward. During treatment, they learn coping mechanisms, develop problem-solving skills, tools to resist cravings, and strategies to regulate their inner world in a better and healthier way without needing to use drugs. Put simply, they need to be protected with strong skills to deal with bumps on the road to recovery and severe weather conditions ahead. The length of the inpatient treatment program usually depends on several factors involving the severity of the addiction, the presence of medical or psychological conditions, and the progress being made. But one thing is clear: A lasting change does not happen overnight. According to the National Institute on Drug Abuse (NIDA), inpatient and outpatient treatments for less than 90 days have proven to be less effective, and longer periods are recommended for success (NIDA 2018). It is quite beneficial to be away from a problematic environment that is full of triggers and cues serving as an invitation for drug use. We sometimes cannot see the bigger picture or the problem in front of us when we are stuck in such a deep hole. Removing everything that reminds us of drug use and its negative influences is a good start to looking back at one's life from a distance and reflecting. New insights, perspectives, ideas, and people in a supportive environment are key ingredients to find the way out of old habits and destructive behavior.

Outpatient Treatment Programs: Outpatient treatment programs are a common form of treatment for teens. They are ideal for those with less severe addictions and fewer additional problems, such as mental health issues. They typically do not require around-the-clock care or monitoring. Outpatient treatment allows people to go about their lives, like attending school and living at home while at the same time continuing their counseling and therapy sessions. This provides them with a natural healing environment with friends and family around. Individuals attend the outpatient program at specific times each week and the skills they learn can be implemented and practiced immediately without any delay. Many begin their recovery journey with inpatient treatment and move to outpatient programs once symptoms ease and significant progress has been made. Yet sometimes it is the other way around. Some start with outpatient treatment and transition to inpatient programs if treatment is not successful and more support and structured care are needed. However, outpatient programs have the benefit that they enable people to practice learned skills in a natural environment and give them the flexibility to balance treatment and other responsibilities. This is also a less expensive treatment option than inpatient or residential programs, making it more accessible and affordable for many.

Behavioral Interventions: Therapies such as cognitive-behavior therapy (CBT), also commonly referred to as talk therapy, can be very beneficial to manage cravings, identify triggers, learn how to manage them, and identify and monitor negative thoughts and behaviors. It helps to develop the skills to change them. Individuals learn to develop strategies on what to do in high-risk situations, learn to use self-control, and learn how to regulate emotions, as well as how to cope with stress. CBT can also help address any underlying issues and improve mental health conditions such as depression and anxiety that may contribute to drug use. CBT is usually offered in residential and outpatient settings as part of group or individual sessions, as a standalone therapy, or as part of a comprehensive treatment program. CBT requires specialized training and is usually provided by a licensed therapist, psychiatrist, or psychologist.

Family Therapy: I highly recommend incorporating family therapy by a licensed family counselor during the recovery treatment. It can help your family move past mistakes and hurt while learning ways to support your child's recovery. This should be a family decision, and everyone involved needs to be on the same page. Not all family members are ready to dig up the past at the same time. You do not want to make things worse by making the emotional wound bleed even deeper. But it can be a valuable treatment option. It can help find any underlying issues that may have contributed to drug use and teach family members, including parents, siblings, grandparents, and close friends, communication skills to improve relationships and aid in recovery. Loved ones learn about the challenges of addiction and the individual's personal struggles which can promote empathy and support from members that can lead to a healthier family dynamic. This is important as teens usually continue to live in the family home. Without addressing problems and improving relationships, things can easily get out of control and fall apart. It can lead to better treatment outcomes for your teen if they feel supported and understood. Family therapy is insufficient as a standalone treatment option to treat addiction, but it can be an ideal addition to a comprehensive treatment plan.

Medication-Assisted Treatment (MAT): There are FDA-approved medications available to treat addictions like alcohol, opioid, and nicotine. For opioid use disorder, methadone, injectable naltrexone, or buprenorphine is currently available. These are especially effective to reduce cravings and withdrawal symptoms and do not produce, contrary to the common misconception, a 'euphoric high'. This can be an effective treatment option for those who cannot or will not want to fully stop opioid use. FDA-approved medications for alcohol use disorders are currently acamprosate, disulfiram, and naltrexone. And for nicotine addiction, the medications bupropion and varenicline are used along with nicotine replacement therapy (i.e., gum, nasal sprays, lozenges, nicotine patches, etc.).

Please note that MAT by itself is insufficient. It is most effective when combined with counseling and behavioral therapy. Individuals reap great benefits from learning skills to manage withdrawal symptoms and cravings, address underlying issues, and develop other life skills to promote long-term abstinence. Especially for opioid addiction, MAT has the benefit of improving quality of life by reducing the risk of overdose, reducing the risk of infectious diseases, improving health, keeping individuals away from criminal activity and the drug scene, and allowing them to have a normal life. Consult with a medical provider who has experience treating adolescent addiction to discuss options for treatment as some MATs are not FDA-approved for individuals under the age of 18.

Extended Care: To maintain the gains made in the treatment, ongoing care is extremely important and necessary. Unfortunately, many skip this step due to overconfidence. They later find themselves struggling when they are out of a therapeutic environment and on their own. They are in an environment that is usually full of triggers and cues. A drug-free life will require continued care. Unlike formal education, recovery is not a school where former substance users graduate and move on. Rather, it is an ongoing process, more like a continued education that lasts a lifetime. Encourage your child to attend a 12-step program like Alcoholics Anonymous (AA) or Narcotics Anonymous (NA). The programs welcome anybody, no matter what stage of their recovery they may be at. Studies show that people who attend self-help programs have a higher success rate in recovery, have fewer cravings, and engage in less risky behavior (Tracy and Wallace 2016, Reif et al., 2014). Being in an environment where fellow recovering individuals share their feelings and struggles is a great encouragement to sustain recovery and prevent relapse. Finding the right peer support groups is like a hit-and-miss game. The energy of the group needs to match the energy of your teen. Allow your child to explore a few groups before making the decision to join one.

7.2. How You Can Finance Addiction Treatment

Addiction treatment can be expensive and a valid concern for many. But there are affordable and even free options available to anyone with a limited economic background. The cost of addiction treatment depends on several factors, such as the type of treatment, location, and length of the treatment program. Here are some common ways people pay for treatment to give you an idea so you can explore your options:

Insurance Plans: Major insurance providers cover all or partially for drug counseling, mental health, and addiction treatment as well as for preventive services. Call your insurance provider and find out what your deductible is and if there are any co-pays or other out-of-pocket costs.

Medicaid: Medicaid is a government-funded health care program that enables individuals' health care based on income and other factors. Medicaid may pay for drug treatment, but it varies state by state which makes it hard to make a general statement. Check with Medicaid in your state and find out if your child is eligible for coverage. Also, not all rehab centers accept Medicaid. If you have Medicaid, look out for a center that does.

Payment Plan: Some treatment programs offer payment plans or have sliding-scale fees. A Sliding-scale fee is a payment system that is based on a person's income, financial resources, and other relevant factors which makes services available to everyone.

Publicly Funded or Non-Profit Organizations: There are publicly funded treatment, non-profit organizations, local support groups, and faith-based organizations that offer help at little to no cost to those with fewer economic resources.

Scholarships: Some institutions offer scholarship programs to help those who lack financial resources for treatment. One such program worth considering is a foundation called 10,000 Beds. They find treatment spots for people in need by partnering with treatment facilities nationwide. The partner facilities 'donate' their open treatment spot but commit to donating at least one treatment scholarship (bed) a year (visit 10000Beds.com to apply). The 10,000 Beds basically connects people who need treatment with the facility. Just in 2021 alone, they were able to provide 1200 scholarships valued at $20,000,000 (10,000Beds 2021).

Private Resources: Some use their own financial resources and pay for the full cost of the treatment out of pocket, in a lump sum, or in installments. For those without insurance coverage, this option may be ideal if you have the means to afford it. You may want to consider taking a home equity loan, borrowing from family or friends, selling your valuables or even using your 401(K). Do not hesitate to use fundraising platforms such as GoFundMe.com or YouCaring.com. Again, a lack of resources should never be the reason for not getting your child into a recovery program. The cost of not receiving the help you need for your child is much higher. Be resourceful and do not make a lack of resources prevent you from getting your child into treatment. I believe in the phrase that 'if there is a will, there is a way'.

7.3. Checklist to Prepare Your Child for Treatment

- **Financial Resources**: How do you plan to cover your treatment? Out of your savings? Personal loan? Insurance plan? Check with your insurance provider to find out your out-of-pocket costs.

- **Treatment Options:** What treatment centers are available in your area that specialize in adolescent drug treatment? Research and visit different centers to find the one that suits your child's needs and also aligns with your budget. Ask them about their recreational activities for teens, scholarship programs, as well as payment plans. Make sure the facility is licensed, accredited, and has a low staff-to-patient ratio. Also, make sure it has a good reputation for working with teens who offer evidence-based and age-appropriate therapies and counseling by experienced staff members. At **Findtreatment.gov** you search for substance use and mental health facilities, health care centers, and MAT practitioners throughout the country.

- **Pick the Right Treatment Center:** You may want to do an orientation beforehand and meet the staff and observe the facility and see if you would feel comfortable and confident about a particular facility. Involve your child actively in the decision-making process and make them pick the option that they are most comfortable with.

- **Fill Out Intake Forms:** Start the process by filling out all the necessary forms and provide the facility with the necessary documents such as medical records and insurance information. It is likely that your child will need to undergo a series of assessments either by the treatment facility or by a qualified mental health provider. This will help identify the severity of addiction, mental health issues, substance use history, family history, and all other relevant factors important for determining the most effective treatment plan for your child.

- **Make Arrangements for Day 1:** Make the entry to treatment as smooth and stress-free as possible. This will likely be an emotional day for both of you as it is a big step toward recovery. You and your teen may feel fear, uncertainty, or anxiety about the road ahead. The onset of treatment also signals the end of suffering. It signals hope for a healthier future and a new beginning. Tell your teen how proud you are and that you will always be there for support throughout the treatment and beyond. Show your excitement and your teen will likely 'catch' your excitement too.

- **Prepare Your Child for Treatment:** Prepare your child mentally for what to expect in treatment including the rules, restrictions, and guidelines of the facility. Set the expectation for how the daily routine will look like and address any concerns, fear, or worry your child may have. Motivate and encourage your child for this journey and make them get excited for the road ahead and all the new people he or she will meet.

- **Plan Transportation:** If your child is attending an outpatient treatment program, plan for how your child will get to the center and back. You can involve friends and family on days you are unable due to other obligations.

- **Pack Your Child's Bag:** Pack your child's bag with all necessary items including clothing, toiletry, or any medications or medical supplies needed. To provide a sense of comfort, emotional support, and familiarity in an unfamiliar setting, you can pack your child's favorite comfort items such as a favorite blanket or pillow, stuffed animal, or pictures of family and friends. Make sure to check with the treatment center to find out what is and is not allowed to be brought in.

- **Plan for Ongoing Care or Education:** It is always advisable to plan ahead. How will subsequent treatment continue after treatment? Counseling, aftercare programs, and support groups are some of the extended care options. There are great school recovery programs that offer education and recovery services at the same time. One such program is called 'Recovery High School'. These are secondary schools designed for students recovering from drug addiction. They offer regular school courses, provide support in their recovery, and students have the opportunity to complete their high school diploma (visit Recoveryschool.org to find a school near you). The Association of Recovery in Higher Education (ARHE) helps students in recovery on college campuses by providing them with resources for academic success and helping them prevent relapse in a supportive environment (visit Collegiaterecovery.org to learn more).

7.4. Do Treatments Actually Work?

Well, it depends. The effectiveness of a treatment program depends on several factors. Let us take a look at some key indicators that can play a key role in a successful treatment:

1. **Quality of Treatment Plan:** Drug addiction is a complex, chronic, and lifelong disease and because everyone carries different risk factors and a history with drugs is different. Therefore, intervention and treatment strategies need to be evidence-based and personalized to the individual's needs. The best treatment plans incorporate different approaches, like using pharmacological intervention (i.e., MAT) in combination with behavioral therapies (i.e., CBT). Medication can help control withdrawal symptoms and cravings while behavioral interventions can help build healthy coping strategies. A comprehensive approach is like a toolbox full of tools. Each tool addresses or 'fixes' a different problem and the use of different tools are more effective than using just one when trying to rebuild a broken structure.

2. **Support System:** The level of support during and after treatment by family or aftercare programs are vital elements for a successful recovery. People in recovery need encouragement, emotional support, practical assistance (i.e., driving to rehab / school / work) and people who hold them accountable. The importance of other resources such as housing, employment, continuing education, and access to health care cannot be underestimated.

3. **Mental Health Problems:** As mentioned previously, if the treatment program fails to address co-occurring mental health issues, it will make it difficult for the person to recover from addiction and sustain abstinence. You can imagine mental health and addiction as two sides of the same coin. You cannot separate them and damage to one side can affect the other.

4. **Motivation to Change:** The belief about the effectiveness of a treatment and their own motivation is key for a positive outcome. The mind is so powerful that it does what it believes. You can guide your teen to treatment and spend thousands of dollars but at the end of the day, if your child doubts the effectiveness and enters treatment with an attitude and perception that it just will not work, it likely will not. Like Henry Ford famously said,

> **Whether you think you can or**
> **you think you can't you're right**

This quote highlights the power of our mindset so well. Our actions and outcomes depend on our beliefs and attitudes. Teens need to have a positive mindset about their recovery and look forward to a better and more prosperous future. If they believe in their success, they will enter treatment committed and determined. They are active participants in their recovery, following their treatment plans and making necessary lifestyle changes. The mindset is the difference between success and failure, and often the difference between recovery and relapse.

We know that drugs affect brain structure and its function. People with an addiction typically have an impaired decision-making capacity the self-control is handed over to drugs. The job of a treatment specialist is to 'fix' or 'rebuild' their willpower. That is the benefit of counseling, therapy, and mentors as positive role models. You too can join this collaborative effort. You can be a part of this process by helping your child develop a 'growth mindset' and resilience. A growth mindset is the belief that with effort, hard work, and determination we can improve our abilities and even our intelligence. This can help them view their addiction or recovery as a temporary setback and not a permanent defeat. It is challenging but doable and achievable. Be patient, empathetic, and supportive. Encourage your child to set goals and celebrate small as well as big victories along the way while viewing obstacles as small bumps on the road to success.

An eternal bond that makes it

through every trial and mistake.

Chapter Eight

MOVING FORWARD

8.1. Helping Your Child on the Journey to Healing

In this chapter, I want to arm you with a few tips to help your child prevent a relapse after the completion of a therapy or a treatment program. Maybe your child's substance use was not severe. Perhaps they made the recovery all on their own simply by changing their behavior. Regardless of how they made the recovery, do not let your guard down. Recovery is one thing, staying sober is completely another. You can play an important role in helping your child prevent relapse to drug use. Here are some tools and strategies on how YOU can support your loved one in this transformative journey and help reduce the chances of relapse:

1. **Provide Emotional Support:** Recovery puts people on a challenging and emotional journey. By providing your support and encouragement your child will feel your genuine love and empathetic presence. But this does not mean that you become a helicopter parent and micromanage your child's life and solve every problem they encounter. Rather, you are to be there as a resource, providing guidance, and only intervening when appropriate. By solving problems and overcoming setbacks, they learn reliance that can serve them well throughout their life.

2. **Encourage Healthy Habits:** It is important to get into the habit of taking care of both body and mind. Encourage your child to prioritize self-care and model healthy habits yourself. Healthy habits can include eating a balanced diet, getting enough sleep, and going to school or work on time.

3. **Set Clear Expectations:** You can be supportive and set clear non-negotiable rules and expectations at the same time. And you can be warm and supportive but still firm. Balance is the key. Make clear that you will not tolerate drug use and that you expect your child to continue treatment, keep appointments and responsibilities, attend ongoing care, and meet obligations. This includes not missing school/work and laying out consequences for any violations such as curfew or losing privileges. Remember the key is to be consistent.

4. **Provide Practical Support:** Practical support includes driving them to school or appointments, helping with school projects, or keeping track of medication intake and schedule. Your child should not depend on you for everything. You do not want to be a crutch. Your well-intended assistance can be counterproductive. Every time you do something for them that they can do for themselves, you deprive them of the chance to become independent, build self-esteem, and master their own life. They must take a certain degree of responsibility and take the steps, no matter how big or small, toward their success and growth. This is for their benefit as much as it is for yours. They simply will not grow their mental muscle if they do not get the opportunity to think for themselves.

5. **Provide Reward and Incentives:** Incentives for hard work always pay off to motivate and encourage staying addiction free. Look for ways to reward your child in big or small ways for hitting milestones. Celebrate your child's progress, milestones, and achievements. It will help build confidence, motivate, and reinforce behavior to continue the recovery process.

6. **Help Them Set Realistic Goals:** Encourage your child to set goals that he or she can work toward with excitement. Make him or her imagine what is truly possible! Make sure that the goal is achievable, measurable, and specific. Setting unrealistic goals can cause a lot of frustration and discourage them from setting new goals in the future. Achieving even small goals is rewarding that can motivate them to move forward toward a brighter and more prosperous future. This can include attending recovery support groups or therapy sessions and aiming for higher degrees or certification.

7. **Keep Your Home Safe and Drug-Free:** Remove all the paraphernalia that was a part of your child's drug use. Monitor closely all prescription medication or even consider locking up the medicine cabinet as a preventive measure. Do not leave pill bottles out around the house. Consider disposing of any harmful medicine that you no longer need. Opioid pain killers having similar chemical properties as street drugs and therefore are addictive, they are used by many as a substitute for street drugs. This also includes the bottle of wine in the cabinet as it can be a trigger for someone trying to remain sober. It is also a good idea to skip a glass of

your favorite alcoholic beverage when you are out for dinner. You probably have seen family members shaving their head when their loved one is battling with cancer and lost all hair. Provide the same emotional support, set clear boundaries in a safe and nurturing space called home. Make it clear to family members and friends that your house is a substance free zone and that includes alcohol, nicotine, etc.

8. **New Cell Phone Number:** This is an important step that is frequently missed. In order to cut ties with drug using peers and drug dealers, get a new cell phone number. It will not only prevent your child from reaching out to them, but it also prevents others associated with drug use from communicating with your child. It is also important for privacy and safety reasons to protect them from harassment from unwanted calls or messages. Even more importantly, a new number also signals a fresh start, leaving old habits and associations behind and proving an even more commitment to a permanent recovery. This also includes emails and if necessary, closing or changing social media accounts. It sounds like a drastic measure but if the purpose and goal is to keep them safe and prevent a relapse, it will be well worth it!

9. **Encourage Physical Social Activities:** Encourage your child to participate in sports that he or she shows an interest in. Research shows that sports can foster positive change in people recovering from an addiction. It enables a sense of belonging, helps transform their identity, and provides the platform to connect with like-minded people with similar values (Landale & Roderick 2013). Besides, it occupies them

with positive and health promoting behavior, leaving less room (and time) for drug promoting behavior.

10. **Healthy Substitutes:** Support your child in identifying and engaging in rewarding activities he or she favors when a craving is triggered. This can be anything, from baking, singing, dancing, taking a walk-in nature, coloring, playing or listening to music, painting, or any other fun activity. Any method to distract their mind from drugs that is within reach in times of urgent need are great coping strategies against craving.

11. **Change the Physical Environment:** You cannot throw your child back into the same environment that broke him or her and that encouraged drug use in the first place. It is not rocket science to predict that if your child starts hanging out with their drug using friends, who have a negative influence on them, he or she is likely to relapse. It may be too much to ask, but I highly encourage you to completely change the environment, ideally to a completely different location. This can be a different neighborhood, different town, or even a different state. My experience has shown that as long as people live in the same household, same environment, or around drug abusing friends, it is nearly impossible to stay sober for very long. It sucks them right back into the old system and their old habits. The environment is full of cues that trigger strong cravings and serve as strong associations to drugs. Even small changes in the environment such as redecorating your child's room or repainting the walls can have a positive effect on their mood and well-being. It can

give them a sense of renewal and signal a new beginning. Any aesthetic change in the environment that promotes relaxation and newness can help break the old pattern and protect against a relapse in a small way. However, it does not replace professional treatment and ongoing care is vital to sustain abstinence.

12. **Address Unresolved Trauma and Mental Health Conditions:** Recovery does not suddenly eradicate underlying trauma and mental health issues. Any lingering symptoms besides addiction can be a danger to recovery. Talk to a qualified healthcare professional to develop a personalized treatment plan that is tailored to your child's needs. As discussed earlier, trauma and mental health conditions can contribute to substance use and can lead to relapse if not properly addressed.

13. **Encourage Ongoing Care:** As discussed in the previous chapter, ongoing care is crucial for their long-term success. Help your child to understand the importance of ongoing continued care. They can be too optimistic and feel on top of the world when things are going well, but they need to be equipped with skills to deal with emotions when they do not.

14. **Avoid Triggers:** Triggers are everywhere and can be everything that reminds them of drug use. It can be people, places, things, or situations. The brain remembers and associates those things with the drug use and every time your child is confronted with them, the brain can ring a loud alarm bell saying 'Oh, I remember you did drugs with this person, this thing, at this exact location etc. That is why it is so

important to abstain from drug using friends. It is best to avoid all triggers, especially at the beginning of the recovery journey, until skills are developed to resist those temptations and urges.

15. **Accountability Buddies/Sponsors/Mentors:** Having an accountability buddy, sponsor, or mentor can be of great help for emotional support and encouragement when the road gets bumpy. Just think of the benefits and wisdom someone who struggled with a former addiction can provide who is way ahead in their own recovery. They can be great role models and a source of inspiration, someone to whom they can relate. People who have successfully overcome an addiction are called sponsors. They can help navigate through the challenges and help them make healthier choices. However, they do not replace professional treatment or therapy but are a great addition to the treatment plan. Sometimes there are things they simply do not feel comfortable talking with parents about, especially when the communications channels between the teen and the parents are not the best. Accountability buddies, sponsors, and mentors can help keep the teen on track with their recovery and make them stay focused on their goals. They usually check on them regularly, hold them accountable for their behavior, and make sure they are not engaged in any risky behavior that could jeopardize their recovery. Being supported by someone outside the family just adds to a strong support system that can be a huge asset for anyone in

their ongoing recovery journey (see also 4.4. on how mentors can guide the way).

16. **Regular Drug Test:** Drug testing your child is a sensitive issue and a mixed blessing. It can be useful and counterproductive at the same time. On the one hand it shows that you mistrust your teen which can damage the relationship. Yet on the other hand it can serve as a useful tool to encourage your child to remain drug free. The benefit of a drug test is to identify quickly in case of a relapse, which allows for swift intervention. Whether to use it or not really depends on individual circumstances. However, instead of using force, have an open conversation with your child and lay out the reason behind your approach.

Please note that every child is different and unique. There is no one-size-fits-all approach when it comes to relapse prevention. Everyone's needs, conditions, and circumstances are different. Be a good listener and observer. Encourage your child to openly communicate their needs so you can provide the best support and environment for their success. Recovery is never complete and people in recovery never arrive at their destination. This does not mean that they have failed or are inadequate. It simply means that healing is a journey. This is true for all of us. Life is a continuous process, and we never reach a finite endpoint where we stop growing and improving. This will be true for as long as we live. Just realizing this fact helps tremendously to keep the focus on the path forward, celebrating victories along the way, and approaching challenges and adversity with a growth mindset.

8.2. Life After Addiction: What to Expect on the Road Ahead

*L*ife in recovery will be full of ups and downs for your teen. Let me remind you at this point that life will never be the same. Not for you, not for your child in recovery, and not for your family. In dealing with the challenges drug abuse brings, everyone changes in the process. That is fine, change is a part of growth. Everyone will have to learn to adapt and create a "new normal" moving forward. If your child is going through some rough times, it can be tempting to assume the worst and come to conclusions without merit. Be patient with your child as they try to process the changes in their identity and their world. They now have to fill the void in their life left by drug use, and this is far from an overnight process. They need space for self-discovery and to reconnect with their authentic self. One of the goals of treatment is to help individuals process their experiences and gain insight into their core values and beliefs. This is exactly why ongoing care is necessary. With structured group and individual therapies, they help in the process of rediscovering one's identity, set goals for the future, and help formulate a relapse prevention plan to cope with cravings and triggers. With the emotional turmoil at times, there are also many positive changes that need to be celebrated. While they are trying to rebuild their health, their life, their academic or work, they may become overwhelmed. But it is very rewarding to witness the transformation. Here are a few potential highlights awaiting you and your teen:

Improving Physical Health: Drugs can really cause a lot of damage to the body. The immune system is weak, is likely to have nutritional deficiency, or even suffer from organ damage. Your child will feel better overall as the body will slowly heal from the damage of substance use. They will have more energy, will sleep better, and start enjoying their food. Make sure you take your child for regular check-ups and monitor that all necessary medications are taken as prescribed by your child's healthcare provider.

Better Mental and Health: That drugs can impact mental health was mentioned many times throughout this book. After abstinence from drugs, your child is likely to experience an improvement in symptoms. This does not mean that he or she will never experience emotional turmoil like anxiety, depression, desperation, or hopelessness.

Improved Relationships: There is no question that addiction strains relationships between friends and family. They can now work on rebuilding the broken ties, make new connections, and form new friendships through support groups or other recovery settings.

Finding a New passion and Purpose: Addiction erases everything that was valuable before and that includes goals and passions as well as a sense of purpose. They can now reignite their old passion, discover new interests, and develop healthy habits to lead a fulfilling life. This includes continuing their education, finding a job, or chasing new goals and dreams.

Increased Confidence: Having their 'normal' life back can help rebuild their confidence, self-esteem, and self-worth. There is no doubt that substance use deteriorates their physical appearance too. Now that they are in recovery, they will start glowing again. Their skin heals from drug related injury, skin clears up from acne, and physical hygiene becomes essential again. This significantly boosts their well-being. I have seen the transformation firsthand. Some former offenders I have later seen out in public were unrecognizably beautiful without drugs and with proper self-love. This is how it looks like to have control of your life back into your hands from using drugs.

Self-Discovery: Now they have to find out who they really are. It is as if they woke up from a long sleep. They can even be happier after recovery than they were before using drugs. Finally, being able to live a normal life like other teens can be an exhilarating experience and the beginning of a life full of gratitude without needing drugs for happiness.

8.3. What if My Child Relapses?

I want to prepare you for the possibility of a relapse. Sometimes it takes a few attempts for a successful and lasting recovery. Remember, addiction is a disease. Just as cancer and heart disease can come back after months or years of recovery, so too does addiction. It can be incredibly difficult for the parent to control their emotions when relapse occurs. My tip: Be kind, patient, and understanding. Do not hold on to resentment or anger and surely do not blame yourself or your child for a failed attempt. It will be a challenging and emotional experience for the individual too. They feel like all the gains and time spent on the treatment have been completely wasted. They may feel shame, guilt, hopelessness, disappointment in themselves and saddened to have let their family down. I would like to remind you that a relapse does not determine your child's worth. Neither is it a sign of weakness. Starting treatment is actually a sign of strength and courage, and relapse, as much as the goal is to avoid it, is way better than not trying at all. Please also remember, the next time he/she will not be starting from zero but from added experience. If your child falls back, encourage him or her to course correct and get back on the road to recovery. They may be tempted to give up and say things like 'I tried, it is not working', 'I simply cannot do this, this is pointless', or 'I am such a loser'. It is really critically important that you offer encouragement and help push them through the challenges. Refer to Dr. Perry's 3'R of communication methods on how to Regulate, Relate, and Reason with your child. Remember, before you try to reason, you need to calm your child down when he or she is emotional or upset. If you find yourself in this situation, here are a few tips to keep in mind:

Stay Calm: It can be a very difficult and emotional experience to learn that your child relapsed. It is also important that you keep calm and not react out of disappointment or anger. Your child may already feel ashamed or guilty and your response can make things worse.

Communicate: Encourage your child to talk about what happened, about his or her feelings, and what caused the relapse. Be understanding and respond with compassion, empathy, love, and support. They need you now more than ever. There is to be no finger-wagging, yelling, screaming, threatening, or cursing. You want to avoid escalating the situation by reacting in a way that scares them or makes them more hostile and defensive. Ask your child what needs to happen for them to get back on the road to recovery. Find out their specific needs so they can be included in the new action plan moving forward. Reassure them that you love him or her no matter what. By staying calm and composed, you are modeling how to handle stressful and difficult situations, and that builds resilience that can help them succeed the next time they need to start their recovery journey once more.

Seek Help: Seek professional help as soon as possible. If your child is already working with a therapist, counselor, or addiction specialist, reach out to them and let them know. Maybe the plan did not work because it was not tailored specifically to your child's needs. This is why it is so important that the treatment plan matches the unique challenges and needs of your teen. Maybe the current plan needs to be changed or adjusted: it needs higher intensity of care, additional support, or monitoring. Also reach out for support for your well-being too. All the negative emotions of stress, anger, and anxiety can take a toll on your physical and mental health and taking care of your needs is part of being an effective and supportive parent. Pause, take a break, breathe, and recharge.

Never Give up: Stay positive and do not give up. It can be tempting to turn away from your child out of exhaustion and you feel like you are at your limit. Just like your love for your child is endless, I am also certain so is your support. No matter the choices your child makes, please know that recovery is not a one-way street. Our children are a part of us – but they are not us. You cannot expect them to do what you would do. It is not reasonable for them to think and feel the way you would think and feel, nor act and behave the way you would act and behave. They are their own being and have free will. You may ask 'At what point is it enough to try to help?'. My answer is 'Never', the answer is to never give up. Just by being your child, they earn the right to unconditional love and support. Never let go of their hand. If they fail, you help them get up. That is what we do, we are their mom.

But what I will suggest is to take care of your well-being and your family and do not neglect your other 'non-using' children's needs. Do not make drug use and bad behavior be the only way to get your attention. We discussed the harmful effects of neglect and negative childhood experiences. While trying to support your child with an addiction, do not be blind to your partners or other needs of your children. The last thing you want is to cause harm to your relationship and other children and multiply the problems. Sometimes life unfolds itself in opposite ways to our expectations and desires. But embrace imperfection and uncertainty because life itself is not perfect and nothing is certain. We are all flawed and imperfect human beings. To expect perfection is the road to unhappiness. It simply truly does not exist. And please do me a favor: Never ever give up hope. Life is full of miracles. As long as your child is breathing, it is never over. There is always hope and the road to recovery is only one decision away.

8.4. Beyond Motherhood: Carve Out Space for the Woman Within

Drug use can have a significant impact on parents. It can be extremely challenging trying to cope and help a child with a substance use problem. In addition, also trying to juggle the responsibilities and commitments of day-to-day life. Managing a household, caring for other family members, making time for your spouse or partner, and work causes an overload on mom's shoulder where her own needs and interests take a back seat. What adds to the stress is the financial burden. Recovery, rehab, and therapy are expensive, which creates additional financial challenges and strain. This challenge is especially difficult for single moms who work long hours to make ends meet. They become so fixated on current circumstances and concerned about the well-being of their loved ones, that they forget about their own needs. No wonder when the only mission becomes to free your child from addiction. With drug use in the family being the problem, deep sadness, anger, fear, or even guilt takes its toll on body and mind. At a time like this when they need all the social support they can get, they become more and more isolated. It is not uncommon for many to withdraw from social activities out of shame and embarrassment. If this sounds like you, I would like to remind you that you deserve to live a happy life and move past the disappointment and hurt caused by your child's drug use or addiction. Self-care is not selfish. Self-care is in fact, self-love. Never feel guilty for taking time for yourself. You might be thinking 'how can I possibly think about myself when my son or daughter is engaging in self-destructive behavior?' Do not fall into the trap of mom guilt. It is actually imperative that you do so. By making time for the woman within you, you can feel recharged and better equipped to deal with the challenges of motherhood. The more energy you have, the more you have to give.

You can help your child, but you will never control him or her. The only person you really have control over is yourself. Therefore, take charge of your health and your well-being, even when things are not working in your favor. Find comfort in the discomfort, the positive in the negative, and joy in joyless circumstances. To be a force for good to others we love, we need to hit the reset button and fill our energy tank. Make time for activities that bring you joy and are relaxing. Some ways to help you recharge include:

1. **Take a Break:** Hit the snooze button from your daily routine and the demands of your environment. This can be journaling, taking a walk, or simply catching up on your sleep. Give yourself permission to rest and rejuvenate.

2. **Do Something Fun:** Leave everything behind and do something that brightens your mood. Engage in activities or a hobby that you are passionate about. For some it is gardening, for others it might be painting, or jogging. What

activity makes you forget time, which feels relaxing and recharging? What can you do today to make yourself feel good? How can you put a pep in your step? What can shift your energy?

3. **Practice Mindfulness:** Meditation or yoga is not only calming and relaxing but also therapeutic. It is proven to reduce stress, anxiety, and worry (Corliss 2014, Hölzel et al. 2010). Give yourself a gift of only ten minutes a day. Simply be present, focus on your breathing, and be in the moment. If your mind starts to wander off, gently bring it back to the center. Carefully observe negative thoughts, feelings, and memories without judgment. Imagine your thoughts as clouds. Let them pass without holding on to them. Visit brightwingsandcoco.com to access a free guided meditation and discover evidence-based tips and strategies to effectively reduce stress and anxiety.

4. **Ask for Support:** Self-care is also asking for help when you need it. Do not be reluctant to reach out to close friends and family for practical support, comfort, or a sympathetic ear. Reach out to a close friend or family member you can confide in for advice or simply connect to enjoy the company of those you care about while giving your mind a break at the same time. Give them a call and schedule a nice evening or a dinner out.

5. **Exercise:** Exercise has numerous benefits for mind and body. Research shows that it can reduce stress, anxiety, and depression (Cooney et al., 2013, Harvard Health Publishing 2020, Mayo Clinic 2017). Even if you do not feel like it, do it

anyway. With exercise, the brain releases the neurotransmitters dopamine, endorphins, and serotonin that will help elevate your mood and sense of well-being. What is your favorite exercise or physical activity? Choose an activity that you enjoy so you can stick with it over time.

6. **Join Parent Support Groups:** I highly recommend joining parent support groups as it will help you learn from the experiences of other parents who are further along in their recovery. Twelve Step meetings, Al-Anon, or Nar-Anon are great sources who welcome family members and provide great support for people struggling with family members addiction. I want you to understand that it is normal to feel exhausted, be at your limit, and drained. People who walked in your shoes with similar challenges can comfort, understand, learn from each other and provide much needed emotional support. Telling your story can be a huge relief as many parents keep the addiction a secret. You never know who you may inspire and touch with your story. Maybe you need professional counseling for your own healing process. Some employers offer access to counseling services or employee assistance programs (EAPs) designed to offer confidential support to employees with mental and emotional issues and help in various challenges. I applaud this win-win effort of those companies and organizations who invest in the well-being of their employees. Whichever option you prefer, whether in person, online, or at work, just get the support you need to address your concerns.

7. **Time to Reconnect:** It can be incredibly stressful and difficult for you and your partner or spouse when dealing with an addiction in the family. It can be draining and overwhelming for both of you. Maybe you recognize that your relationship suffered due to dealing with current life events and that it is now the time to reconnect. If a relationship suffers during this time, it just adds to the stress you already have. Great ways to reconnect are date nights, having deep conversations, and hearing each other out. If you think things have gotten out of hand, you may consider couple's therapy. While it is the intention of this book to empower you, remember that you are ultimately stronger as a team. You can navigate this crisis much better with a strong support system and your significant other can be an essential part of it.

8. **Think of Lessons Learned:** I know it is hard or even unimaginable to look for positives and the lessons learned in tough circumstances. But there is always something we all learn from adversity and harsh experiences. Some people become less judgmental, become wiser, more tolerant, choose compassion, and appreciate the little things in life even more. What are the lessons you have learned? In what positive ways did this experience change you for the better?

8.5. Overcoming Stigma: Let People Talk. Who Cares?

If only everything was as simple as it looks from the outside. Nobody that walks in your shoes knows how the rocky road of drug addiction feels. As if going through this challenging time is not enough to deal with, people face negative judgments and stigmatization by society because of their association with drugs. This becomes an unnecessary but larger barrier for parents and substance users to seek help. You would assume (at least we hope) that healthcare professionals provide the same care for everybody and treat them equally. Unfortunately, they too carry a stigma toward people suffering from drug addiction and this has impacted the level of healthcare service they provided (Van Boekel et al., 2013). Dr. Bruce D. Perry, psychiatrist and neuroscientist, says it beautifully. He made in his joint book with Oprah Winfrey 'What Happened to You? Conversations on Trauma, Resilience and Healing' the following remark:

"Marginalized people---excluded, minimized, shamed---are traumatized people... humans are fundamentally relational creatures. To be excluded or dehumanized in an organization, community, or society you are part of results in prolonged, uncontrollable stress that is sensitizing... Marginalization is a fundamental trauma" (2021, p. 220).

I could not agree more. By excluding, minimizing, and shaming them, we are only making the problem worse. When humiliation and shame are too big, drug use becomes a family secret until the problem becomes so big until it is no longer hidden. **My advice to parents: Let people talk. Do not concern yourself about your reputation or social status. The only thing you should be concerned about is you and your loved one's**

health and well-being. Do not fall prey to comparing your child to your neighbor's son or daughter who seems to be the 'perfect' child. I can see your head nod in recognition. I know we are all guilty of this. We compare ourselves to others, our children to the children of others, our job, education, or our economic status. Nobody wins the comparison game. Comparison is the thief of joy. It drains our mental energy that we need for our priorities. Addiction can happen to anyone. No matter what car they drive, how much money they have, their sexual orientation, or their gender. Because drugs are a social problem. One problem that we face is the unequal treatment of people who use legal versus illegal drugs. The society stigmatizes those who are addicted to illegal drugs as it is often associated with criminal activity, violence, and addiction. Legal drugs, on the other hand, are accepted or even encouraged in certain social context. Legal drugs are perceived as safe and harmless despite mountains of evidence of their harmful effects. Alcohol, for example, is such a big part of our leisure and social life, that hardly any social gathering is organized without some kind of alcoholic beverages. It is simply ingrained in our culture and associated with fun that it is almost a violation of a social rule if you do not drink along with the group. It seems that the governmental regulation and control of substances creates the false sense of safety that seems to make a difference in people's perception instead of judging it by its potential for harm and abuse. This highlights two goals: First, to destigmatize those addicted to illegal drugs, so they overcome the inhibition to seek help. Secondly, to raise awareness to the fact, that the term 'legal' does not eradicate the harm legal drugs like alcohol, cigarettes, and prescription drugs can cause. They are as harmful and addictive as illegal drugs as we have already discussed in this book.

What about the impact of social media? Commercials and social media can influence teens and how they perceive legal drugs making it appear normal to use them. With all the suggested solutions to cope with any imaginable human problem possible. You got a headache? Take this! Do you suffer from depression? Take that! Do you want to be cool? Drink this! Instead of helping them learn coping mechanisms, they may turn to legal drugs as a quick fix to the problem. With all this temptation around us, it is hard to blame our vulnerable young minds for stepping into the landmine of substance abuse. But how can you protect your child from the negative influences of people, social media, marketing gurus, and drugs? One solution is since we cannot influence and eradicate what is happening outside, we need to empower them from the inside. One way to do this is to disempower the effect outside influences by, for instance, is to help them develop the ability to take a critical perspective when they encounter media messages. You can make comments like "'they do not really care about your well-being." Or "They just want your money." Something like, "notice the background music to influence your emotions". Or perhaps say something like "why are the tobacco and alcohol industry targeting younger generation in their ads? Because older people who are hooked already figured out that it was a mistake, are sick, or dead!". What you are doing is planting a seed in your child's mind. They cannot 'unhear' what you said, and they will soon be thinking about it the next time they see or hear a sales pitch. We need to teach our children to care less about the noise that want our attention and our money and care more about our own well-being. Knowledge is power. Educate yourself so you can pass it on to your loved ones.

We also have to raise awareness to the fact that substance use disorder is a brain disease. People do not understand how drugs hijack the brain and how difficult it is for those struggling with an addiction to quit. I truly believe that helping people who suffer from an addiction is our moral obligation. We need to ask ourselves why we come up short as a society. Do the youth have opportunities and resources to spend their leisure time in their communities? Do the youth have access to a quality education, workforce, counseling or are drugs their only option to earn, belong, and cope? Let us begin by eliminating a few words from our vocabulary when referring to individuals who struggle with an addiction. Words matter. The White House released a memorandum called *Changing the Language of Addiction* proposing to use proper terminology around substance use that is neutral and non-stigmatizing (Botticelli 2017). I like their recommendation to use first-person language like 'a person in recovery' instead of 'clean' because it implies that people in recovery are somehow dirty. It also recommends using phrases like 'person with a substance use disorder' or 'person with an alcohol use disorder' instead of 'substance abuser', 'addict', or 'alcoholic'. Words matter. Derogative terms only lead to stigma, negative stereotypes, and shame that is offensive, humiliating, and harmful. People with drug addiction are not bad people.

Many experienced trauma and neglect and/or lacked the positive environment and role models. It leads them to make poor decisions like using drugs to meet their emotional need. We must not take away their humanity. As an inspiration, the acronym L-O-V-E can help you take steps to reduce stigmatization in your community:

L—Listening: Encourage others to take the time to listen to the stories of others around addiction without judging or stereotyping. By actively listening, we can understand their challenges and perspectives, promote empathy, and learn ways to encourage and support them in their journey to recovery. Behind every story is a human being with a unique story and their own unique experiences, emotions, and thoughts. By listening to others, we not only demonstrate that we care and value them as a person but also help build a more compassionate and empathetic society.

O—Open-Mindedness: Be open about your own experience with addiction or that of a loved one. By sharing your personal story, you make a difference by helping others affected by addiction. It can give someone the hope, strength, and motivation needed to reach out for help without feeling shame and be willing to break their own silence.

V—Value of Community: Helping people get out of an addiction is a collective effort. You can help reduce stigma by raising awareness in your community by speaking up, advocating for policies and programs, and spreading the word about this disease. In the end, addiction is a social problem. Everyone is affected by it, directly or indirectly. By raising awareness, we can reduce the stigma around addiction and help open the gateway for those in need to reach out for help without fearing judgment and discrimination.

E-Educate Yourself: Educate yourself about addiction so you can help and support your loved one more effectively and use your knowledge to educate others in the community. By reading this book, you now have the information needed and are in a position to help others understand this disease better, help reduce stigma, and promote a better understanding of drug addiction.

As you can see, love can solve so many of the problems that we deal with in our society. It comes in many forms, from listening, showing kindness, encouraging, and supporting those in need, whether we know them or not. The language of love is universal and knows no culture, religion, or race. Everyone deserves respect and empathy and is worthy of receiving care and attention for a healthy and prosperous life. Beginning today, let us begin by encouraging and supporting those who struggle with addiction. Today, begin to help the often marginalized and overlooked. Let us follow the principles and guidelines that are set forth in the United States Declaration of Independence, adopted on July 4th, 1776. It states that *"all men are created equal"* *(National Archives 2022)*. Another important guideline comes from the Universal Declaration of Human Rights, adopted by the United Nations General Assembly in 1948. It states that *"the inherent dignity and of the equal and inalienable rights of all members of the human family is the foundation of freedom, justice, and peace in the world."* *(United Nations 1948)*.

Let us come together and strive to uphold the principles of equality and connect with those in need with more compassion, respect, and love. Let us teach others how to harvest tolerance, peace, and acceptance, along with mutual understanding. Let us lead by example and create a culture of support and unity and take those in need under our wings.

CONCLUSION

This book has come to an end, but your journey to help your child out of an addiction may just be beginning. Every single day is an opportunity to start again and to choose again. A new day to choose recovery, a new day to quit drugs, to be a better parent, to choose actions toward new goals and dreams. Use the practical suggestions and tools that resonate with you the most and simply disregard the rest. One size does not fit all when it comes to strategies and tactics. But when it comes to love and connection, one size always fits all. Positive relationships are a strong buffer and can counterbalance adversity. No matter where you and your child are on your journey, do not underestimate the impact of your love and support. It can heal all wounds because love is a powerful antidote to drugs. Love makes forgiveness possible, clearing the rubble of past hurts caused by addiction and paving the road to an amazing future that awaits.

Take care of yourself. The stronger and healthier you are physically and emotionally, the more energy you will have for your family. Drop the backpack filled with negativity and replace it with gratitude, grace, and appreciation. Focus on the light in the darkness. Sometimes things need to fall apart to give birth to a better, stronger, and wiser YOU. Never forget that you are allowed to be upset, scream at the top of your lungs, and cry all you want. But after a minute or two, get a hold of your composure and straighten back your crown. You are a mom, a queen, the leader, the backbone, and a forgiver. The one who fixes broken hearts and wings and the super-glue that holds the family together when things seem to fall apart. You are a mom, working around the clock, selfless for the well-being of the entire family. A mom that deserves the best, a life without suffering. An amazing mom for just holding this book in your hands to find the right answers to your questions.

May this book empower you with much insight, hope, comfort, and wisdom. It was my honor to offer you guidance and tips to guide your loved one away from addiction. It is my sincere wish, with your love and support and the support of professionals, that your child will overcome this challenge and take the first steps to freedom to have an amazing and prosperous life thereafter. May you draw upon the currency of your heart to guide, protect, and inspire your loved one on this journey through life. Remember that you are a warrior, and your love is your weapon in this victorious battle.

With love and gratitude,
Nevriye A. Yesil

ABOUT THE AUTHOR

Nevriye Yesil was born in 1976 in Hamburg, Germany. She holds a Masters' Degree in Forensic Psychology. She is the author of two other books (in the German language) published in Austria, Germany, Switzerland, and Luxemburg, one on Brainpower and High-performance skills 'Kanck Dein Gehirn fur Deinen Erfolg' (2019) and one on drug addiction 'Drogen Haben Kurze Beine' (2021). She is currently running a successful coaching business, Bright Wings & Coco, LLC, and helps families all over the world to cope with drug addiction. She advises moms and mentors teen to a successful life. A fun fact about her is that she is a competitive athlete in Olympic weightlifting and earned the German Masters Weightlifting Championship in 2022. Nevriye has two kids, Tamara and Matthew, and currently lives in Alabama with her cats.

Acknowledgments

I am filled with gratitude for the people who have helped me along the way. First and foremost, I would like to express my gratitude to my mentors and teachers, who have inspired me with their knowledge, guidance, and wisdom. Their passion for their respective fields and dedication have had a profound impact on my intellectual growth.

My sincere gratitude to Tony Robbins & Sage Robbins who taught me the importance of service, impact, and contribution.

Thank you to my platinum friends and success coaches Lisa Lieberman-Wang, Sys Savanth, JJ Villar, Rob Purcell, David Leiter, Kiana Danial, Consuelo Villar, Joaquin Fava Aguiar, Erwan Le Roy, Katy Peters, Victoria Jancke, Noam Zimin, Marc Anthony, Henrike Schelper, Daniel Matuschzik, Jenn Allen, Riya Arora, Sherman Ewing, my chosen brother Arber Balidemaj, and all other platinum brothers and sisters I forgot to mention. I cannot put into words how much your wisdom and friendship have added to my life.

I also owe a debt of gratitude to Robert J. Bolton for your editing and Dani Popova for the beautiful cover design. Thank you to my weightlifting coach and Olympian Michaela Breeze for pushing me beyond my limits. My special friends who bring so much joy into my life, Karen Pugh, Wendy Hunter, Sheila Haile, Kristy Cook, Isin Engin, and Nalan Sengezer, my BFF for over 35 years.

And finally, I would like to thank my readers, whose interest and enthusiasm for this book have been a source of motivation and inspiration. I hope that the ideas presented in this book will be of value to you and I wish you and your family all the best on this journey to recovery.

Dear Mom,

Thank you for your courage to jump on the train and leave poverty behind. You saved us all. To my father: I wish you could see your little girl thrive. I love and miss you both. To my brother and sisters who always remind me that we are all one. My children, Tamara and Matthew, I am the wealthiest person because of you two. I would like to express my gratitude to Sadik Yesil, for the impact he had on my life. Your presence has always been valued and I am grateful for your continued presence and support. My furry babies are Oreo and Peynir. I wish you guys knew how much you are loved.

Life is happening for me and not to me. And so, it is.

Sincerely,
Nevriye A. Yesil

REFERENCES

1. Understanding Substance Use and Addiction

1.1. Chaos of Drugs on the teen brain

Di Chiara, G., & Imperato, A. (1988). Drugs abused by humans preferentially increase synaptic dopamine concentration in the mesolimbic system of freely moving rats. *Proceedings of National Academy of Sciences of the United States of America, 85*(14), 5274-5278. https://doi.org/10.1073/pnas.85.14.5274

Franklin, T., Acton, P. D., Maldjian, J. A., Gray, J. D., Croft, J. R., Dackis, C. A., O'Brien, C. P., & Childress, A. R. (2002). Decreased gray matter concentration in the insular, orbitofrontal, cingulate, and temporal cortices of cocaine patients. *Biological Psychiatry, 51*(2), 134-142. https://doi.org/10.1016/S0006-3223(01)01269-0

Gould, T. J. (2010). Addiction and cognition. *Addiction Science & Clinical Practice, 5*(2), 4-14.

Hamilton, P. J., & Nestler, E. J. (2019). Epigenetics and addiction. *Current Opinion in Neurobiology, 59,* 128-136. https://doi.org/10.1016/j.conb.2019.05.005

Han, B., Compton, W. M., Einstein, E. B., Cotto, J., Hobin, J. A., Stein, J. B., & Volkow, N. D. (2022). Intentional drug overdose deaths in the United States. *The American Journal of Psychiatry, 179*(2), 163-165. https://doi.org/10.1176/appi.ajp.2021.21060604

Jordan, C. J., & Andersen, S. L. (2017). Sensitive periods of substance abuse: Early risk for the transition to dependence. *Developmental Cognitive Neuroscience, 25*, 29-44. https://doi.org/10.1016/j.dcn.2016.10.004

Lyoo, I. K., Pollack, M. H., Silveri, M. M., Ahn, K. H., Diaz, C. I., Hwang, J., Kim, S. J., Yurgelun-Todd, D. A., Kaufman, M. J., & Renshaw, P. F. (2006). Prefrontal and temporal gray matter density decreases in opiate dependence. *Psychopharmacology, 184*, 139-144. https://doi.org/10.1007/s00213-005-0198-x

Mooney-Leber, S. M., & Gould, T. J. (2018). The long-term cognitive consequences of adolescent exposure to recreational drugs of abuse. *Learning & Memory, 25*(9). 481-491 https://doi.org/10.1101/lm.046672.117

National Institute on Drug Abuse. (2023, February 9). *Drug overdose death rates.* https://nida.nih.gov/research-topics/trends-statistics/overdose-death-rates

National Institute of Mental Health. (2023). *The teen brain: 7 things to know.* https://www.nimh.nih.gov/health/publications/the-teen-brain-7-things-to-know

National Institute of Mental Health. (2023, March). *Substance use and co-occurring mental disorders.* https://www.nimh.nih.gov/health/topics/substance-use-and-mental-health

The National Child Traumatic Stress Network. (2008, June). *Making the connection: Trauma and substance abuse.* https://www.nctsn.org/sites/default/files/resources/making_the_connection_trauma_substance_abuse.pdf

Nicolas, C., Tauber, C., Lepelletier, F. X., Chalon, S., Belujon, P., Galineau, L., & Solinas, M. (2017). Longitudinal changes in brain metabolic activity after withdrawal from escalation of cocaine self-administration. *Neuropsychopharmacology, 42*, 1981-1990. https://doi.org/10.1038/npp.2017.109

Pérez-Ramírez, Ú., Díaz-Parra, A., Ciccocioppo, R., Canals, S., & Moratal, D. (2017). Brain functional connectivity alterations in a rat model of excessive alcohol drinking: A resting-state network analysis. *39th Annual International Conference of the IEEE Engineering in Medicine and Biology Society (EMBC)*, 3016-3019. https://doi.org/10.1109/EMBC.2017.8037492

Vetreno, R. P., Yaxley R., Paniagua, B., Johnson, G. A., & Crews, F. T. (2017). Adult rat cortical thickness changes across age and following adolescent intermitted ethanol treatment. *Addiction Biology, 22*(3), 712-723. https://doi.org/10.1111/adb.12364

Volkow, N. D., Koob, G. F., & McLellan, A. T. (2016). Neurobiologic advances from the brain disease model of addiction. *New England Journal of Medicine, 374*(4), 363-371. https://doi.org/10.1056/nejmra1511480

1.2. Ticking time bomb: The path to addiction

Everitt, B. J., & Robbins, T. W. (2013). From the ventral to the dorsal striatum: Devolving views of their roles in drug addiction. *Neuroscience & Biobehavioral Reviews, 37*(9, Part A), 1946-1954. https://doi.org/10.1016/j.neubiorev.2013.02.010

Schoenbaum, G., & Shaham, Y. (2008). The role of orbitofrontal cortex in drug addiction: A review of preclinical studies. *Biological Psychiatry, 63*(3), 256-262. https://doi.org/10.1016/j.biopsych.2007.06.003

1.3. What is an addiction anyways?

National Institute on Drug Abuse. (2020). *Drug misuse and addiction.* Drugs, brains, and behavior: The science of addiction. https://nida.nih.gov/publications/drugs-brains-behavior-science-addiction/drug-misuse-addiction

Hasin, D. S., O'Brien, C. P., Auriacombe, M., Borges, G., Bucholz, K., Budney, A., Compton, W. M., Crowley, T., Ling, W., Petry, N. M., Schuckit, M., & Grant, B. F. (2013). DSM-5 criteria for substance use disorders: Recommendation and rationale. *American Journal of Psychiatry, 170*(8), 834-851. https://doi.org/10.1176/appi.ajp.2013.12060782

1.4. Why drug addiction is a brain disease

Volkow, N. D., & Koob, G. (2015). Brain disease model of addiction: Why is it so controversial? *Lancet Psychiatry, 2*(8), 677-679. https://doi.org/10.1016/S2215-0366(15)00236-9

Volkow, N. D., Koob, G. F., & McLellan, A. T. (2016). Neurobiologic advances from the brain disease model of addiction. *New England Journal of Medicine, 374*(4), 363-371. https://doi.org/10.1056/nejmra1511480

1.5. The healing power of the brain

Garavan, H., Brennan, K. L., Hester, R., & Whelan, R. (2013). The neurobiology of successful abstinence. *Current Opinion in Neurobiology, 23*(4), 668-674. https://doi.org/10.1016/j.conb.2013.01.029

2. Hidden Dangers and False Promises of Drugs

2.1. Lying chemicals: The deceptive nature of drugs

Merriam-Webster. (2023). *Dictionary by Merriam-Webster.* https://www.merriam-webster.com/dictionary/

2.2. Debunking lies about legal drugs

Anstey, K. J., von Sanden, C., Salim, A., & O'Kearney, R. (2007). Smoking as a risk factor for dementia and cognitive decline: A meta-analysis of prospective studies. *American Journal of Epidemiology, 166*(4), 367-378. https://doi.org/10.1093/aje/kwm116

Camchong, J., Lim, K. O., & Kumra, S. (2017). Adverse effects of cannabis on adolescent brain development: A longitudinal study. *Cerebral Cortex, 27*(3), 1922-1930. https://doi.org/10.1093/cercor/bhw015

Centers for Disease Control and Prevention (2022, October 26). *Underage drinking*. https://www.cdc.gov/alcohol/fact-sheets/underage-drinking.htm

Doll, R., Peto, R., Boreham, J., & Sutherland, I. (2004). Mortality in relation to smoking: 50 years' observations on male British doctors. *BMJ, 328*, 1519. https://doi.org/10.1136/bmj.38142.554479.AE

El-Hellani, A., El-Hage, R., Baalbaki, R., Salman, R., Talih, S., Shihadeh, A., & Saliba, N. A. (2015). Free-base and protonated nicotine in electronic cigarette liquids and aerosols. *Chemical Research in Toxicology, 28(8)*, 1532-1537. https://doi.org/10.1021/acs.chemrestox.5b00107

Drug Enforcement Administration. (2021, October 29). *How opioid (painkiller) abuse can lead to heroin use*. Get smart about drugs. https://www.getsmartaboutdrugs.gov/content/how-opioid-painkiller-abuse-can-lead-heroin-use

Goriounova, N. A., & Mansvelder, H. D. (2012). Short-and long-term consequences of nicotine exposure during adolescence for prefrontal cortex neuronal network function. *Cold Spring Harbor Perspectives in Medicine, 2*(12), a012120. https://doi.org/10.1101/cshperspect.a012120

Kandel, E. R., & Kandel, D. B. (2014). A molecular basis for nicotine as a gateway drug. *New England Journal of Medicine, 371*(10), 932-943. https://www.nejm.org/doi/full/10.1056/NEJMsa1405092

Lee, G. A., & Forsythe, M. (2011). Is alcohol more dangerous than heroin? The physical, social and financial costs of alcohol. *International Emergency Nursing, 19*(3), 141-145. https://doi.org/10.1016/j.ienj.2011.02.002

Mayo Clinic. (2022, March 3). *Over-the-counter laxatives for constipation: Use with caution*. https://www.mayoclinic.org/diseases-conditions/constipation/in-depth/laxatives/art-20045906

McCrae, J. C., Morrison, E. E., MacIntyre, I. M., Dear, J. W., & Webb, D. J. (2018). Long-term adverse effects of paracetamol–a review. *British Journal of Clinical Pharmacology, 84*(10), 2218-2230. https://doi.org/10.1111/bcp.13656

Meier, M. H., Caspi, A., Ambler, A., Harrington, H., Houts, R., Keefe, R. S., McDonald, K., Ward, A., Poulton, R., & Moffitt, T. E. (2012). Persistent cannabis users show neuropsychological decline from childhood to midlife. *Proceedings of the National Academy of Sciences, 109*(40), E2657-E2664. https://doi.org/10.1073/pnas.1206820109

Mons, U., & Kahnert, S. (2019). Neuberechnung der tabakattributablen Mortalität–Nationale und regionale Daten für Deutschland. *Das Gesundheitswesen, 81*(1), 24-33. https://doi.org/10.1055/s-0042-123852

National Institute on Drug Abuse. (2019). *Cannabis (marijuana) DrugFacts.* https://nida.nih.gov/publications/drugfacts/cannabis-marijuana

Ngo, V. T. H., Bajaj, T. (2020). *Ibuprofen.* StatPearls Publishing. Retrieved March 31, 2020, from https://www.ncbi.nlm.nih.gov/books/NBK542299/

National Institute on Alcohol Abuse and Alcoholism (2023). *Alcohol facts and statistics.* https://www.niaaa.nih.gov/publications/brochures-and-fact-sheets/alcohol-facts-and-statistics

Sakhuja, A., Sztajnkrycer, M., Vallabhajosyula, S., Cheungpasitporn, W., Patch, R., III, & Jentzer, J. (2017). National trends and outcomes of cardiac arrest in opioid overdose. *Resuscitation, 121*, 84-89. https://doi.org/10.1016/j.resuscitation.2017.10.010

Shmerling, R. (2019). *Can vaping damage your lungs? What we do (and don't) know.* Harvard Health Publishing. Retrieved January 6, 2020, from https://www.health.harvard.edu/blog/can-vaping-damage-your-lungs-what-we-do-and-dont-know-2019090417734

Thomes, P. G., Rasineni, K., Saraswathi, V., Kharbanda, K. K., Clemens, D. L., Sweeney, S. A., Kubik, J. L., Donohue, T. M., & Casey, C. A. (2021). Natural recovery by the liver and other organs after chronic alcohol use. *Alcohol Research: Current Reviews, 41*(1), 05. https://doi.org/10.35946/arcr.v41.1.05

Vonmoos, M., Hulka, L. M., Preller, K. H., Minder, F., Baumgartner, M. R., & Quednow, B. B. (2014). Cognitive impairment in cocaine users is drug-induced but partially reversible: Evidence from a longitudinal study. *Neuropsychopharmacology, 39*(9), 2200-2210. https://doi.org/10.1038/npp.2014.71

2.3. Myth busting facts about drugs

American College of Cardiology. (2017, May 30). *Stopping drug abuse can reverse related heart damage.* https://www.acc.org/about-acc/press-releases/2017/05/30/09/59/stopping-drug-abuse-can-reverse-related-heart-damage

Johnson, K. C. (2018). Just one cigarette a day seriously elevates cardiovascular risk. *BMJ, 360,* k167. https://doi.org/10.1136/bmj.k167

Lambert, N. M., McLeod, M., & Schenk, S. (2006). Subjective responses to initial experience with cocaine: an exploration of the incentive–sensitization theory of drug abuse. *Addiction, 101*(5), 713-725. https://doi.org/10.1111/j.1360-0443.2006.01408.x

Runegaard, A. H., Jensen, K. L., Wörtwein, G., & Gether, U. (2019). Initial rewarding effects of cocaine and amphetamine assessed in a day using the single-exposure place preference protocol. *European Journal of Neuroscience, 50*(3), 2156-2163. https://doi.org/10.1111/ejn.14082

Tyson, T. L., Feick, N. H., Cravalho, P. F., Flynn-Evans, E. E., & Stone, L. S. (2021). Dose-dependent sensorimotor impairment in human ocular tracking after acute low-dose alcohol administration. *The Journal of Physiology, 599*(4), 1225-1242. https://doi.org/10.1113/JP280395

Uusitupa, M., Khan, T. A., Viguiliouk, E., Kahleova, H., Rivellese, A. A., Hermansen, K., Pfeiffer, A., Thanopoulou, A., Salas-Salvadó, J., Schwab, U., & Sievenpiper, J. L. (2019). Prevention of type 2 diabetes by lifestyle changes: A systematic review and meta-analysis. *Nutrients, 11*(11), 2611. https://doi.org/10.3390/nu11112611

2.4. Identifying underlying needs and emotions

Cunningham, K. J. (2018). *The road less stupid: Advice from the chairman of the board.* Keys to the Vault.

3. Power of Genetics and Environment

3.1. The link between Mental Health and Substance use

Kelly, T. M., & Daley, D. C. (2013). Integrated treatment of substance use and psychiatric disorders. *Social Work in Public Health, 28*(3-4), 388-406. https://doi.org/10.1080/19371918.2013.774673

Santucci, K. (2012). Psychiatric disease and drug abuse. *Current Opinion in Pediatrics, 24*(2), 233-237. https://doi.org/10.1097/MOP.0b013e3283504fbf

Silverman, B. C., Najavits, L. M., & Weiss, R. D. (2016). Co-occurring substance use disorders and other psychiatric disorders. In A. H. Mack, K. T. Brady, S. I. Miller, & R. J. Frances (Eds.), *Clinical Textbook of Addictive Disorders* (4th ed.; pp. 292-326). The Guilford Press.

The National Child Traumatic Stress Network. (2008, June). *Making the connection: Trauma and substance abuse.* https://www.nctsn.org/sites/default/files/resources/making_the_connection_trauma_substance_abuse.pdf

Watkins, A., John, A., Bradshaw, C., Jones, J., & Jones, M. (2019). Schizophrenia in high risk opioid users: A short communication on an autopsy study. *Psychiatry Research, 276*, 112-114. https://doi.org/10.1016/j.psychres.2019.04.026

3.2. The role of Genes in the World of Drugs

Goldberg, L. R., & Gould, T. J. (2019). Multigenerational and transgenerational effects of paternal exposure to drugs of abuse on behavioral and neural function. *European Journal of Neuroscience, 50*(3), 2453-2466. https://doi.org/10.1111/ejn.14060

Kendler, K. S., Sundquist, K., Ohlsson, H., Palmér, K., Maes, H., Winkleby, M. A., & Sundquist, J. (2012). Genetic and familial environmental influences on the risk for drug abuse: A national Swedish adoption study. *Archives of General Psychiatry*, *69*(7), 690-697. https://doi.org/10.1001/archgenpsychiatry.2011.2112

Wanner, N. M., Colwell, M. L., & Faulk, C. (2019). The epigenetic legacy of illicit drugs: Developmental exposures and late-life phenotypes. *Environmental Epigenetics*, *5*(4), dvz022. https://doi.org/10.1093/eep/dvz022

3.3. Environmental factors leading to drug use

Pelletier, K. R. (2018). *Change your genes, change your life: Creating optimal health with the new science of epigenetics*. Origin Press.

Pinel, C., Prainsack, B., & McKevitt, C. (2018). Markers as mediators: A review and synthesis of epigenetics literature. *BioSocieties*, 13, 276-303. https://doi.org/10.1057/s41292-017-0068-x

Zimić, J. I., & Jukić, V. (2012). Familial risk factors favoring drug addiction onset. *Journal of Psychoactive Drugs*, *44*(2), 173-185. https://doi.org/10.1080/02791072.2012.685408

3.4. How personal factors can shape addiction

Cheetham, A., Allen, N. B., Whittle, S., Simmons, J. G., Yücel, M., & Lubman, D. I. (2012). Orbitofrontal volumes in early adolescence predict initiation of cannabis use: A 4-year longitudinal and prospective study. *Biological Psychiatry*, *71*(8), 684-692. https://doi.org/10.1016/j.biopsych.2011.10.029

Ersche, K. D., Jones, P. S., Williams, G. B., Turton, A. J., Robbins, T. W., & Bullmore, E. T. (2012). Abnormal brain structure implicated in stimulant drug addiction. *Science*, *335*(6068), 601-604. https://doi.org/10.1126/science.1214463

González Ponce, B. M., Díaz-Batanero, C., del Valle Vera, B., Dacosta-Sánchez, D., & Fernández-Calderón, F. (2019). Personality traits and their association with drug use and harm reduction strategies among polysubstance users who attend music festivals. *Journal of Substance Use, 25*(2), 177-185. https://doi.org/10.1080/14659891.2019.1672818

3.5. Horrors of adverse Childhood experiences

Felitti, V. J. (2003). Origins of addictive behavior: Evidence from a study of stressful childhood experiences. *Praxis der Kinderpsychologie und Kinderpsychiatrie, 52*(8), 547-559.

Nakazawa, D. J. (2015). *Childhood disrupted: How your biography becomes your biology, and how you can heal.* Atria Books.

Perry, B. D. (2002). Childhood experience and the expression of genetic potential: What childhood neglect tells us about nature and nurture. *Brain and Mind, 3*(1), 79-100. https://doi.org/10.1023/A:1016557824657

4. Leading by example

4.1. Why being a good role model is important

Czeisler, M. É., Lane, R. I., Petrosky, E., Wiley, J. F., Christensen, A., Njai, R., Weaver, M. D., Robbins, R., Facer-Childs, E. R., Barger, L. K., Czeisler, C. A., Howard, M. E., & Rajaratnam, S. M. (2020). Mental health, substance use, and suicidal ideation during the COVID-19 pandemic—United States, June 24–30, 2020. *Morbidity and Mortality Weekly Report, 69*(32), 1049-1057.

Ingram, I., Kelly, P. J., Deane, F. P., Baker, A. L., Goh, M. C., Raftery, D. K., & Dingle, G. A. (2020). Loneliness among people with substance use problems: A narrative systematic review. *Drug and Alcohol Review, 39*(5), 447-483. https://doi.org/10.1111/dar.13064

Novotney, A. (2019). Continuing education the risks of social isolation. *Monitor on Psychology, 50*(5), 32-37.

Spitz, R. A. (2017). Hospitalism: An inquiry into the genesis of psychiatric conditions in early childhood. *The Psychoanalytic Study of the Child*, 1(1), 53-74. https://doi.org/10.1080/00797308.1945.11823126

4.2. Riding the Waves: Building Resilience Through Self-Love

Cialdini, R. B., Eisenberg, N., Green, B. L., Rhoads, K., & Bator, R. (1998). Undermining the Undermining Effect of Reward on Sustained Interest. *Journal of Applied Social Psychology*, *28*(3), 249-263. https://doi.org/10.1111/J.1559-1816.1998.TB01705.X

Cialdini, R. B. (2021). *Influence: The psychology of persuasion*. Harper Business.

CNN Business. (2018, March 30). *Spanx founder: My dad encouraged me to fail* [Video]. YouTube. https://www.youtube.com/watch?v=_TeV9op6Mp8

Koob, G. F., & Schulkin, J. (2019). Addiction and stress: An allostatic view. *Neuroscience & Biobehavioral Reviews*, *106*, 245-262. https://doi.org/10.1016/j.neubiorev.2018.09.008

Shoaib, A., Mansoor, A., & Saeed, N. (2018). Stress, anxiety and depression as a predictor in relapse of drug dependence. *Annals of PIMS*, *14*(2), 123-126. https://doi.org/10.48036/apims.v14i2.88

4.3. Correcting our wrongs

Chakravarthy, B., Shah, S., & Lotfipour, S. (2013). Adolescent drug abuse - Awareness & prevention. *Indian Journal of Medical Research*, 137(6), 1021-1023.

Kepple, N. J. (2018). Does parental substance use always engender risk for children? Comparing incidence rate ratios of abusive and neglectful behaviors across substance use behavior patterns. *Child Abuse & Neglect*, *76*, 44-55. https://doi.org/10.1016/j.chiabu.2017.09.015

Yap, M. B., Cheong, T. W. K., Zaravinos-Tsakos, F., Lubman, D. I., & Jorm, A. F. (2017). Modifiable parenting factors associated with adolescent alcohol misuse: A systematic review and meta-analysis of longitudinal studies. *Addiction*, *112*(7), 1142-1162. https://doi.org/10.1111/add.13785

4.4. How mentors can guide the way

Office of Juvenile Justice and Delinquency Prevention. (2020). *Mentoring for preventing and reducing substance use and associated risks among youth.* https://ojjdp.ojp.gov/library/publications/mentoring-preventing-and-reducing-substance-use-and-associated-risks-among

5. How to raise Drug-free children in a Drug-filled World

5.1. The Art of listening and connecting with your child

Amaro, H., Sanchez, M., Bautista, T., & Cox, R. (2021). Social vulnerabilities for substance use: Stressors, socially toxic environments, and discrimination and racism. *Neuropharmacology*, *188*, 108518. https://doi.org/10.1016/j.neuropharm.2021.108518

Campbell, J. A., Walker, R. J., & Egede, L. E. (2016). Associations between adverse childhood experiences, high-risk behaviors, and morbidity in adulthood. *American Journal of Preventive Medicine*, *50*(3), 344-352. https://doi.org/10.1016/j.amepre.2015.07.022

Substance Abuse and Mental Health Services. (2022, October 27). *"Talk. They Hear You."*®Campaign. https://www.samhsa.gov/talk-they-hear-you

5.2. Educate yourself on the harm of substance use

Drug Enforcement Administration. (2023, March 3). *One pill can kill.* Get Smart About Drugs. https://www.getsmartaboutdrugs.gov/content/one-pill-can-kill

Drug Enforcement Administration. (2023, February 15). *Fake pills: What you need to know.* Get Smart About Drugs. https://www.getsmartaboutdrugs.gov/family/counterfeit-pills-what-you-need-know

5.3. Help built and nurture positive relationships

Kelly, J. (2021, December 2). *Peers or parents? Study shows strong friendships set teens up for success later in life.* UVA Today. https://news.virginia.edu/content/peers-or-parents-study-shows-strong-friendships-set-teens-success-later-life

Weir, K. (2012). The pain of social rejection. *Monitor on Psychology, 43*(4), 50.

https://www.apa.org/monitor/2012/04/rejection

5.4. The Cost of Negative Friendships

Branstetter, S. A., Low, S., & Furman, W. (2011). The influence of parents and friends on adolescent substance use: A multidimensional approach. *Journal of Substance Use, 16*(2), 150-160. https://doi.org/10.3109/14659891.2010.519421

6. Breaking the Cycle of Addiction

6.1. Recognize drug use and take Action fast

Belcher, H. M., & Shinitzky, H. E. (1998). Substance abuse in children: Prediction, protection, and prevention. *Archives of Pediatrics & Adolescent Medicine, 152*(10), 952-960. https://doi.org/10.1001/archpedi.152.10.952

Chakravarthy, B., Shah, S., & Lotfipour, S. (2013). Adolescent drug abuse - Awareness & prevention. *Indian Journal of Medical Research, 137*(6), 1021-1023.

6.2. Confrontation: Help your child to say YES to recovery

Perry, B. D., & Winfrey, O. (2021). *What happened to you? Conversations on trauma, resilience, and healing.* Flatiron Books.

6.3. Evidence-based approaches to motivate behavior change

Garrett, J., & Landau, J. (2010). *ARISE to help your family member recover from alcohol, drug, and other addictions: A proven intervention and lifelong recovery guide for families.* Taylor & Francis.

Hétu, S., Grégoire, M., Saimpont, A., Coll, M. P., Eugène, F., Michon, P. E., & Jackson, P. L. (2013). The neural network of motor imagery: An ALE meta-analysis. *Neuroscience & Biobehavioral Reviews, 37*(5), 930-949. https://doi.org/10.1016/j.neubiorev.2013.03.017

Landau, J., & Garrett, J. (2008). Invitational intervention: The ARISE model for engaging reluctant alcohol and other drug abusers in treatment. *Alcoholism Treatment Quarterly, 26*(1-2), 147-168. http://dx.doi.org/10.1300/J020v26n01_08

6.4. The double-edged sword of using force

National Institute on Drug Abuse. (2018, January). *Principles of drug addiction treatment: A research-based guide* (3rd ed.). https://nida.nih.gov/sites/default/files/675-principles-of-drug-addiction-treatment-a-research-based-guide-third-edition.pdf

7. Treatment options and recovery for teens

7.1. Common treatment options to overcome addiction

National Institute on Drug Abuse. (2018, January). *Principles of drug addiction treatment: A research-based guide* (3rd ed.). https://nida.nih.gov/sites/default/files/675-principles-of-drug-addiction-treatment-a-research-based-guide-third-edition.pdf

Reif, S., Braude, L., Lyman, D. R., Dougherty, R. H., Daniels, A. S., Ghose, S. S., Salim, O., & Delphin-Rittmon, M. E. (2014). Peer recovery support for individuals with substance use disorders: Assessing the evidence. *Psychiatric Services, 65*(7), 853-861. https://doi.org/10.1176/appi.ps.201400047

Tracy, K., & Wallace, S. P. (2016). Benefits of peer support groups in the treatment of addiction. *Substance Abuse and Rehabilitation, 7*, 143-154. https://doi.org/10.2147/SAR.S81535

7.2. How you can finance addiction treatment

10,000 Beds (2021). *10,000 beds: One bed, one life.* https://10000beds.org

8. Moving Forward

8.1. Helping your child on the healing journey

Landale, S., & Roderick, M. (2014). Recovery from addiction and the potential
role of sport: Using a life-course theory to study change. *International
Review for the Sociology of Sport, 49*(3-4), 468-484.
https://doi.org/10.1177/1012690213507273

8.4. Beyond Motherhood: Carve out space for the woman within

Cooney, G. M., Dwan, K., Greig, C. A., Lawlor, D. A., Rimer, J., Waugh, F. R.,
McMurdo, M., & Mead, G. E. (2013). Exercise for depression. *Cochrane
Database of Systematic Reviews.*
https://doi.org/10.1002/14651858.CD004366.pub6

Corliss, J. (2014, January 8). *Mindfulness meditation may ease anxiety, mental
stress.* Harvard Medical School.
https://www.health.harvard.edu/blog/mindfulness-meditation-may-
ease-anxiety-mental-stress-201401086967

Harvard Health Publishing (2020, July 7). *Exercising to relax.*
https://www.health.harvard.edu/staying-healthy/exercising-to-relax

Hölzel BK, Carmody J, Evans KC, Hoge EA, Dusek JA, Morgan L, Pitman RK,
Lazar SW (2010) Stress reduction correlates with sturctural changes in
the amygdala. Social Cognitive and Affective Neuroscience 5(1):11-17.
https://doi.org/10.1093/scan/nsp034

Hölzel, B. K., Carmody, J., Evans, K. C., Hoge, E. A., Dusek, J. A., Morgan, L.,
Pitman, R. K., & Lazar, S. W. (2010). Stress reduction correlates with
structural changes in the amygdala. *Social Cognitive and Affective
Neuroscience, 5*(1), 11-17. https://doi.org/10.1093/scan/nsp034

Mayo Clinic (2017, September 27). *Depression and anxiety: Exercise eases symptoms.* https://www.mayoclinic.org/diseases-conditions/depression/in-depth/depression-and-exercise/art-20046495

8.5. Overcoming Stigma: Let people talk. Who cares?

Botticelli, M. P. (2017, January 9). *Changing the language of addiction.* Office of National Drug Control Policy. https://obamawhitehouse.archives.gov/sites/whitehouse.gov/files/images/Memo%20-%20Changing%20Federal%20Terminology%20Regrading%20Substance%20Use%20and%20Substance%20Use%20Disorders.pdf

National Archives (2023). *The declaration of independence.* Retrieved March 20, 2023, from https://www.archives.gov/founding-docs/declaration

Perry, B. D., & Winfrey, O. (2021). *What happened to you? Conversations on trauma, resilience, and healing.* Flatiron Books.

United Nations (1948). *Universal declaration of human rights.* https://www.un.org/en/about-us/universal-declaration-of-human-rights

Van Boekel, L. C., Brouwers, E. P., van Weeghel, J., & Garretsen, H. F. (2013). Stigma among health professionals towards patients with substance use disorders and its consequences for healthcare delivery: systematic review. *Drug and Alcohol Dependence, 131*(1-2), 23-35. https://doi.org/10.1016/j.drugalcdep.2013.02.018

OTHER PUBLICATIONS BY THE AUTHOR

https://tinyurl.com/yvnmmy75   https://tinyurl.com/yecd9r6f   https://tinyurl.com/y7bmw5sw   https://tinyurl.com/vkt94ec3

https://tinyurl.com/yc6hu4yn   https://tinyurl.com/5yujb7nn   https://tinyurl.com/2p8c8zru   https://tinyurl.com/2p9ww9x2

www.ingramcontent.com/pod-product-compliance
Lightning Source LLC
Chambersburg PA
CBHW050340160726
48002CB00001B/393